THEMATIC UNIT
Colonial America

Written by Mary Ellen Sterling, M. Ed.

Teacher Created Resources, Inc.
6421 Industry Way
Westminster, CA 92683
www.teachercreated.com

©1995 Teacher Created Resources, Inc.
Reprinted, 2005

Made in U.S.A.

ISBN-1-55734-597-X

Illustrated by
Karon Walstad

Edited by
Stephanie Buehler

Cover Art by
Sue Fullam

Table of Contents

Introduction

Colonial America contains a unique whole-language, thematic unit about the era when the colonists exhibited great faith and courage. The eighty reproducible pages hold diversified lesson plans designed to use with intermediate and junior high school students. The unit centers around two notable literature selections by Newbery Award-winning authors: *The Serpent Never Sleeps* and *The Witch of Blackbird Pond*. For each of these novels, activities have been created to set the stage for reading, to foster enjoyment of the book, and to extend the concepts which have been presented.

In addition, the unit is thematically connected to the curriculum through activities in language arts (including daily writing activities), math, science, social studies, art, music, and life skills. Many of these activities encourage cooperative learning.

Unit management tools—including suggestions, bulletin board ideas, and reading response journal ideas—give students the opportunity to unify their knowledge into products that can be shared both within and outside the classroom.

This thematic unit includes:

- **literature selections**—summaries of two books with related lessons that cross the curriculum

- **planning guides**—suggestions for sequencing lessons each day of the unit

- **poetry**—suggested selections and lessons enabling students to write their own works

- **writing ideas**—writing activities across the curriculum

- **bulletin board ideas**—suggestions and plans for student-created bulletin boards

- **curriculum connections**—in language arts, math, science, social studies, art, music, and life skills

- **group projects**—to foster cooperative learning

- **culminating activities**—which require students to synthesize their learning and produce products that can be shared with others

- **a bibliography**—that suggests additional literature and nonfiction books on the theme

---

To keep this valuable resource intact so that it can be used year after year, you may wish to punch holes in the pages and store them in a three-ring binder.

Introduction *(cont.)*

Why Whole Language?

A whole language approach involves children in using all modes of communication: reading, writing, listening, observing, illustrating, experiencing, and doing. Communication skills are interconnected and integrated into lessons that emphasize the whole of language rather than isolating its parts. The lessons revolve around the selected literature. Reading is not taught as a separate subject from writing and spelling, for example. A child reads, writes, speaks, listens, etc., in response to a literature experience introduced by the teacher. In this way, language skills grow naturally, stimulated by involvement and interest in the topic at hand.

Why Thematic Planning?

One very useful tool for implementing an integrated whole language program is thematic planning. By choosing a theme with correlating literature selections for a unit of study, a teacher can plan activities throughout a day that lead to a cohesive, in-depth study of the topic. Students will be practicing and applying their skills in meaningful contexts. Consequently, they will tend to learn and retain more. Both teachers and students will be freed from a day that is broken into unrelated segments of isolated drill and practice.

Why Cooperative Learning?

Along with academic skills and content, students need to learn social skills. No longer can this area of development be taken for granted. Students must learn to work cooperatively in groups in order to function well in modern society. Group activities should be a regular part of school life, and teachers should consciously include social objectives as well as academic objectives in their planning. For example, a group working together to write a play may need to select a leader. The teacher should make clear to the students and monitor the qualities of good leader-follower interaction just as he or she would state and monitor the academic goals of the project.

The Serpent Never Sleeps

by Scott O'Dell

Summary

The year is 1609 and Serena Lynn, a headstrong seventeen-year-old English girl, is in love with the controversial Anthony Foxcroft. Her writing skills earn her an invitation to serve King James I at court, but she abandons this opportunity to follow Anthony to Virginia. Since Anthony's mother is a key investor in the London Company, she wants her son to escort the new settlers and supplies to Jamestown. After the *Sea Venture* becomes shipwrecked off the coast of Bermuda, the crew rebuilds and flounders on to Virginia, only to find it in ruins. The survival of the crew and colony lies with Serena and her ability to smooth relations with Pocahontas and her tribe. Without food and supplies from the Indians, Jamestown cannot endure another long winter.

This outline is a suggested plan for using the various activities that are presented in this book. You should adapt these ideas to fit the needs of your students and your classroom situation.

Sample Plan

Lesson 1

- Set the stage. (pages 6-7)
- Locate the place connected to the novel.
- Research the life of King James I.
- Read chapters 1-3 and write in response journals (page 17).
- Plan a masque. (page 11)
- Research an historical figures. (page 26–27)

Lesson 2

- Read Chapters 4-6 and write in response journals (page 17).
- Listen to some colonial music.
- Create character webs. (page 19)
- Study the Great Arcade. (page 12)
- Conduct "Drake's Raid." (page 24)
- Continue to research historical figures.

Lesson 3

- Read Chapters 7-9 and write in response journals (page 17).
- Draw a map of the *Sea Venture's* route.
- Investigate St. Elmo's Fire. (page 12)
- Build a water still. (page 24)
- Learn about the signs of the zodiac. (page 12)
- Continue to research historical figures.

Lesson 4

- Read Chapters 10-13 and write in response journals (page 17).
- Research coral reefs. (page 12)
- Continue to research historical figures.

Lesson 5

- Read Chapters 13-15 and write in response journals (pages 17-18).
- Use describing words in Word Bank. (page 16)
- Research and compare the Calvinist and the Puritan religions.
- Make a mnemosynon. (page 28)
- Continue to research historical figures.

Lesson 6

- Read Chapters 16-19 and write in response journals (page 18).
- Investigate the life of Pocahontas. (page 21)
- Complete the Pocahontas Crossword Puzzle. (page 22)
- Make a coat of arms. (page 13)
- Sing "Frog Went a Courtin'." (page 9)
- Solve text-related word problems. (page 23)
- Share research projects on historical figures.

Lesson 7

- Read Chapters 20-23 and write in response journals (page 18).
- Learn how to play blindman's buff. (page 29)
- Discuss and compare current and colonial penal codes. (page 13)
- Make currant pound cake or Indian pudding. (page 30)
- Draw Indian sign language figures. (page 14)
- Share historical figure research projects.

Lesson 8

- Read Chapters 24-27 and write in response journals (page 18).
- Write appropriate titles for each chapter.
- Read about author Scott O'Dell. (page 31)

Overview of Activities

SETTING THE STAGE

Before embarking on an exploration of Colonial America, you may want to set the stage with one or more of the following projects. Most are ongoing activities that can be continued throughout this unit of study.

1. **Questions.** Attach a large sheet of butcher paper to a classroom wall. Ask the students to share some questions they may have about the colonial period of American history. With a colored marking pen, list the questions on the prepared wall, leaving room for an answer. As you progress through your studies and find answers, write them with differently colored pens.

2. **Webbing.** Create a web on Colonial America. Brainstorm some ideas with the whole group and write the students' responses on spokes radiating from the center. As the unit of study progresses, check off those areas which have been covered.

3. **Museum.** Tell the students they are going to make a mini-museum of the colonial era in America. Each group of students will need to seal a large cardboard box and cover it with butcher paper. After researching the following six topics, students will draw and write about their findings on the six faces of the box: (1) *fashions;* (2) *music, sports and games*; (3) *inventions;* (4) *the economy;* (5) *politics*; and (6) *religion.* Display the finished cardboard projects; allow time for groups to visit the other museums.

4. **Colonial Alphabet Book.** You will need 26 large sheets of tagboard. Label the top of each sheet with a different letter of the alphabet. Punch two holes at the top corners of each page and attach a reinforcement to both sides of each hole. As students learn new colonial words, they can add them to the pages of the alphabet book. A definition and a picture should accompany each entry. When all the pages have been completed, they should be alphabetized and tied together with string or heavy yarn. Display the book in your classroom library.

5. **World Map.** Display a world map throughout the unit to point out locations important to the story. (For this and other activities in the unit, a reproducible world map is provided on page 10.) Trace the route traveled in the novel, beginning at Plymouth, England; then to the Canary Islands; to the west coast of Africa; to Bermuda; and, finally, to Virginia. Pair the students and have them draw and label their own map of this route. Extension: Compare this route with the one traveled by Columbus in 1492.

6. **About Colonial America.** The setting of *The Serpent Never Sleeps* is the early 1600s in Virginia during a severe winter that took the lives of many early settlers. Learn more about this era; highly recommended are Anne McGovern's *If You Lived in Colonial Times* (Scholastic, 1964) and *Colonial American Home Life* by John F. Warner (Franklin Watts, 1993).

Overview of Activities *(cont.)*

SETTING THE STAGE *(cont.)*
---

7. **View a film.** See suggestions on page 80, display pictures, and read historical accounts and journals about the times. See *Constance: A Story of Early Plymouth* by Patricia Clapp (Penguin, 1987). Sing some traditional songs such as "Yankee Doodle" or "America." See *I Love America! A Treasury of Popular Stories, History, Poems, and Songs*, ed. by Shelagh Canning (Western Publishing Company, 1990).

8. **More Questions.** Brainstorm a list of questions about colonial life in Virginia and the Jamestown settlement. Keep this list on display and add questions as you progress through this unit. Write answers to the questions as they are discovered.

ENJOYING THE BOOK
---

1. **Note Taking.** Begin reading *The Serpent Never Sleeps*. Take notes on life in a large, English castle. Use them to compare with what you learned about life aboard a crowded ship.

2. **List of Characters.** Keep an ongoing list of characters as they first appear in the story. Record words and phrases to describe the characters and their relationships to each other (see Character Roster, page 20). As an alternative, list the Jamestown colony leaders. Document each man's strengths, weaknesses, and reason(s) for returning to England. Evaluate which leader contributed the most to the colony and justify your choice.

3. **Analysis.** At the end of each chapter, have the students write a one-paragraph synopsis that describes the action in that section. As a group, analyze the main event for each chapter. Divide students into small cooperative groups and have them design a mural to depict each chapter's content. If preferred, make a quilt rather than a mural, with each student designing an individual patch. Sew the patches together and display the finished quilt.

4. **Vocabulary Development.** A number of methods for developing and strengthening vocabulary skills can be found on page 15. In addition, a suggested Colonial Word Banks can be found on page 16. Add to these banks as you go through the unit.

5. **Reading Response Journals.** Have the students keep Reading Response Journals. Students can make their own by stapling sheets of writing paper together. Choose from either the Chapter Vocabulary and Activities (pages 11-14) or the topics found on pages 17-18.

6. **Research.** Choose a colonial personality to research. Suggested subjects and projects can be found on pages 26 and 27. This can be done individually or in small groups.

King James I of England   Sir Francis Drake   John Rolfe   John Calvin

Sir Walter Raleigh   Pocahontas

Shakespeare   Captain John Smith   Governor Dale   Lord De La Warr

---

Overview of Activities *(cont.)*

7. **Modern Masque.** Discuss the masque being planned by Countess Diana. Talk about its theme and its appropriateness. Ask students to suggest themes for a modern day masque and then set up cooperative groups to devise plans. Tell them to determine an event in history to celebrate, and to create invitations, make decorations, and plan refreshments.

8. **About Pocahontas.** Learn about Pocahontas using the information provided on page 21. Follow up with the Pocahontas crossword puzzle on page 22.

9. **Character Web.** Explore the feelings between characters with a character web. Ask students to describe how two of the characters felt toward one another. Compare two more characters and continue in the same manner until all relationships have been examined. Pair the students to work on a feelings web of their own. See page 19 for suggestions.

10. **Opinions.** Discuss early views on smoking, particularly those held by King James I. Compare his views with current information about smoking and health. Hold a class debate on the pros and cons of smoking. Poll the students and find out how many think it is okay to smoke and how many are against smoking. Make a graph of the poll results.

11. **Word Problems.** Solve the word problems found on page 23. With the whole class, discuss and establish what the problem is asking, what operation is needed to solve each problem, and what clues helped them determine how to find a solution. Students can work individually or with a partner to find solutions. Correct the work together and call on students to explain how they arrived at their answers.

12. **Science.** When the colonists arrived on the island of Bermuda, they found themselves without safe drinking water. A solar still would have enabled them to collect water. Build a solar still using the plans found on page 24.

13. **Art.** Discuss the word "mnemosynon" and how one was constructed before colonists left the island of Bermuda. Students can make a mnemosynon or create a Native American mask. Directions for both of these art activities can be found on page 28.

14. **Pastimes.** Find out what colonial children did during their leisure time. Play some common games of the era, i.e., hopscotch, tag, or blindman's buff, or learn how to embroider. These games and an easy paper-and-pencil embroidery project are described on page 29.

15. **What's Cooking?** Colonists had to adapt to the new foods that they were able to gather in the New World. Thanks to the Native Americans, they were introduced to corn, a food staple in every household. One popular corn dish was Indian pudding. Learn how to make this and currant pound cake with the recipes on page 30.

EXTENDING THE BOOK

1. **Sequel.** Imagine that Scott O'Dell has written a sequel to *The Serpent Never Sleeps*. The setting for the second novel is Virginia in 1634; Tom and Serena Barlow have been married for twenty years. Speculate and discuss aspects of their life at this time. What has happened during the twenty years of their marriage? What have been their accomplishments? What problems do they face now?

Overview of Activities *(cont.)*

EXTENDING THE BOOK *(cont.)*

2. **"Invest in Jamestown".** Promote Jamestown for prospective investors. Let students work in cooperative groups to plan an advertising campaign to market this colonial real estate. They can design posters or radio or television ads. Have the groups take turns presenting their ads to the rest of the class.

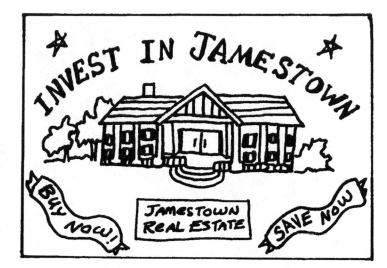

3. **A Star Is Born.** Discuss the character of Emma Swinton in the novel and analyze the author's reasons for placing her in the story. Compare her personality to a similar character in another book or movie. Suggest well-known actresses who could play her part if the novel were to be made into a movie.

4. **Story Elements.** Review the elements of a story—setting, characters, problem, climax, and solution. Attach a large sheet of butcher paper to the wall and make a story elements chart. List the proper information on the chart. Utilizing all of this information, have pairs or groups of students create a story board for *The Serpent Never Sleeps*.

5. **Colonial American Songs.** Have students research and learn some Colonial American songs such as "Frog Went a Courtin'." Practice those which tell a story or correlate with a well-known song; share them in small groups or with the entire class.

6. **Dramatization.** Work in small cooperative groups and discuss favorite scenes from the book. Select one scene to enact; write a script. Groups can take turns presenting the dramatizations to the rest of the class.

7. **Sing It.** Assign students to work in cooperative groups to write a song about a character or characters from the book. Instruct them to take a well-known tune and write new lyrics for it.

8. **Growth.** Examine the population growth of the Virginia colony and compare its expansion with the other colonies. Make a graph or chart of your findings.

9. **What Else?** Make a list of any other questions you have about colonial life in Virginia that the novel may have left you wondering about. For answers, write a letter with your questions to the Historian, Jamestown-Yorktown Foundation, Jamestown Settlement, P.O. Drawer JK, Williamsburg, Virginia 23187.

10. **About the Author.** Read about author Scott O'Dell on page 31. Let students choose and read one of his other novels.

World Map

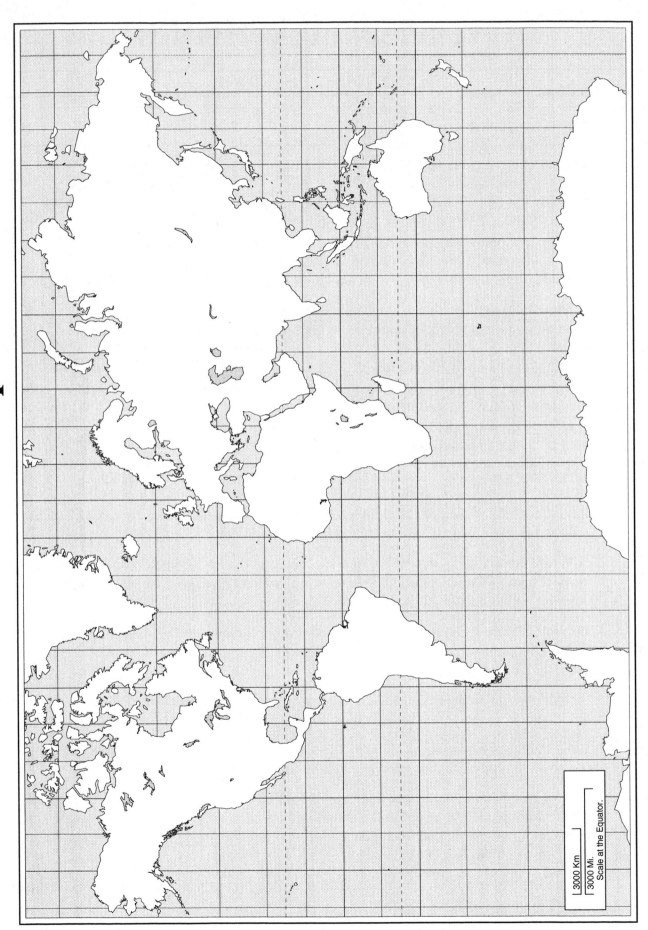

3000 Km

3000 Mi.

Scale at the Equator.

Chapter Vocabulary and Activities

Here through page 14, you will find vocabulary words and activities for each chapter of *The Serpent Never Sleeps*. Vocabulary development activities can be found on page 15.

=================================== **Chapter 1** ===================================

poaching   lopped   contemptuous   infernal   stout   timothy   roily
clacker   flusher   burr   dejectedly   cloister   ponderous

Activity: Read this conversation between the flusher and Serena: "You seem but little interested in the fishing sport," the flusher said. "To me, 'tis not a sport. I'm sorry for the fish. I prefer to let them stay where they be." Direct the students to write a response to this conversation and share it with a partner. With the whole class, discuss students' views about vegetarianism and killing animals for meat.

=================================== **Chapter 2** ===================================

lithesome masque grenadiers bonny libeling conspirators transpires allays   doublet arrogant
fulsome   retainers talisman   albeit churl   transfixed   ascension pavilions victuals varlets

Activity: When the King asks Serena to write to him about the masque, she reveals that she was born left-handed but was forced to use her right hand. Invite students to copy Serena's words on page 9, using their nonwriting hands.

=================================== **Chapter 3** ===================================

boon   daubed   swoon   sultry   amends   piebald   horde   vermin   provisions   feigning

Activity: In this chapter, the countess is planning a masque to raise funds for the Jamestown colony. Direct students to plan a contemporary masque. After deciding on a theme, they will need to plan a guest list, menu, appropriate music, location for the event, and an invitation. Let groups take turns sharing their masque plans with the whole class.

=================================== **Chapter 4** ===================================

cavalcade convey livery bleat trestles scullery wench admonitions cunning cordovan

Activity: Read the description of both the old and new racks on page 29. Draw a picture of each contraption. Write a paragraph to explain how they work. Research other means of punishment used during this era. Would students characterize these methods as humane or inhumane? Discuss.

=================================== **Chapter 5** ===================================

antagonists   sullen   pinnacles   semblance   endeavors   dour   discern
daunt   parley   thither   monologue   incarnadine   eloquent   dithered

Activity: What were King James I's views on the "latest fad" of smoking? What has modern medical research proven about smoking? Conduct a class debate in which panelists discuss the pros and cons of smoking.

Chapter Vocabulary and Activities *(cont.)*

═══════════════════════════ **Chapter 6** ═══════════════════════════

arcade   conceit   crescent   revelry   posthaste   eminent   fetes

Activity: Read the description of Countess Diana's "sweet conceit," the Great Arcade. Have the class plan and draw a mural or make scale models of the arcade.

═══════════════════════════ **Chapter 7** ═══════════════════════════

fortnight   hindrance   quay   sauntered   pinnacles

Activity: When Reverend Bucke learns Serena intends to travel on the *Sea Venture,* he asks her if she has given any thought to the hardships she might encounter. With a partner, make a list of possible hardships on board a seventeenth century ship; compare with ocean travel today.

═══════════════════════════ **Chapter 8** ═══════════════════════════

pious   gilded   lubberly   evasive   incessant   privateers   plaudits   brackish   durance

Activity: Serena's birthdate is May 23, making her a Gemini. Consult an astrological chart and let the students find out their signs. Learn the twelve signs of the zodiac and the symbols and personality traits associated with each month. Follow the astrological guides posted in the local newspaper for a week.

═══════════════════════════ **Chapter 9** ═══════════════════════════

tumult   bilge   roster   coaxed   oakum   ballast
sugar-loaf hat   offing   withering   waning   rue   encumbered

Activity: Research the phenomenon known as St. Elmo's Fire. Find out the difference between these lights and the Northern Lights and Southern Cross. Where are you most likely to find these lights? Draw a picture of what the lights around a ship's mast might look like.

═══════════════════════════ **Chapter 10** ═══════════════════════════

conjured   ample   marooned   meager   condescended   berth

Activity: Ask students what they know about coral reefs. Record responses on the board or chart paper. Have them research how coral reefs are formed and add the new information to the chart.

═══════════════════════════ **Chapter 11** ═══════════════════════════

conspirators   galleon   demeanor   breach   ceased   deem   bounties   folly

Activity: Tom wades into a cave and finds a huge lobster. Build a life-size papier mâché model of this lobster, using a chicken wire frame, or draw the huge lobster.

═══════════════════════════ **Chapter 12** ═══════════════════════════

manacled   concoction   depose   pallor   heedless   halcyon   covenant   revoke   tumult   preening

Activity: Reread Reverend Bucke's speech to the camp on page 78 of the novel. Write your own speech that you would make to encourage everyone to help rebuild.

═══════════════════════════ **Chapter 13** ═══════════════════════════

menial   duress   banished   parlous   transparent   shoals   wisps

Activity: Admiral Somers decided to make a chart of all the islands and reefs as well as the wildlife he encountered. Have students draw a map of the nearly one hundred islands and islets he encountered.

Chapter Vocabulary and Activities *(cont.)*

═══════════════════════════ **Chapter 14** ═══════════════════════════

strode   hewers   loyalists   ruse   hurled   scoffing   brazenly   tunny

Activity: Men in Bermuda worked slowly on new ships because they knew that, once built, they would encounter the scarcity of the New World. With a partner, list the pros and cons of staying in Bermuda versus leaving for the colonies. If you were Serena Lynn, what would you choose to do and why?

═══════════════════════════ **Chapter 15** ═══════════════════════════

dissenters   viola   mnemosynon   dipsey   fathoms   descried   debris

Activity: *Deliverance* and *Patience* had to wait for a westerly wind before they could channel into the sea. Have the students research and draw a globe with names and directions of prevailing winds in both hemispheres.

═══════════════════════════ **Chapter 16** ═══════════════════════════

hillock   sprightly   desolation   bevy   stentorian   famine   pestilence
despot   confederacy   indulge   whim   dubious   domain   smitten

Activity: Chief Powhatan ruled 28 tribes that inhabited Virginia. Group the students; provide each group with a current map of the state in order to list the Indian names they can locate.

═══════════════════════════ **Chapter 17** ═══════════════════════════

brandished   deportment   dialect   invocations   werowance   phalanx
effigy   sullen   defied   appeased   scanty

Activity: Tell students that Pocahontas is the first person their own age that they have seen in many months. Instruct them to write a conversation they might have with her (she can speak your language fluently). Let students work with a partners to practice and perform conversations.

═══════════════════════════ **Chapter 18** ═══════════════════════════

dissenting   fusillade   cudgeled   kindled   dire   waistcloth

Activity: An English coat of arms was displayed on the largest ship. Have students research coats of arms and the figures that appear on them. Then they can design their own coat of arms. (See *Kids' America* by Stephen Caney, Workman Publishing, 1978.)

═══════════════════════════ **Chapter 19** ═══════════════════════════

loomed liveried commission bulwarks   exempt harangued teemed   garrison
hapless evoke calamity impoverishment persist flourish happenstance lofty

Activity: Admiral Somers' cabin was decorated with scenes of Neptune and his court of sea nymphs. Have students research Neptune and his myth. Draw and decorate a wall similar to the one seen in Admiral Somers' cabin.

═══════════════════════════ **Chapter 20** ═══════════════════════════

resolve   bided   florid-faced   faltering   appalled
proclamation   martial law   culprits   wield   sect

Activity: Offenses and punishments imposed by Sir Thomas are listed on page 30 of the book. Let groups of students make posters of classroom offenses and appropriate punishments; have them draw comparisons between current penal laws in their area and those laid down by Sir Thomas.

Chapter Vocabulary and Activities *(cont.)*

=== Chapter 21 ===

| consumed | dubious | frolicsome | fraught | quarry | trepidation |
| brook | disciplinarian | vapors | heedless | heathenish | rite |

Activity: Serena learns some Indian language and signs from the captives at the fort which she eagerly shows Marshal Dale. Direct the students to draw their own signs, plus five more items of their choice. Share the pictures in small groups.

=== Chapter 22 ===

| minions | confound | coup | ninny | convey | ruse | quell |

Activity: Serena escapes when she suspects that Captain Argall will capture Pocahontas. Do you think Captain Argall's plan is a good one? Why or why not? With a partner, devise a back-up plan Argall should have had ready in case his first one failed.

=== Chapter 23 ===

| pall | wrath | rash | vague | regally | loath |

Activity: With Pocahontas safely on board, Captain Argall does all he can to make her comfortable. Because she is curious, Pocahontas and Serena talk about England. Write a letter to Pocahontas giving answers to her questions. Share the completed letters in the whole group.

=== Chapter 24 ===

| resplendent | meager | ransomed | pallet | relented | swooningly | apparition | boisterous | staid |

Activity: When Tom Barlow is hit by an arrow, the wound becomes infected, and Pocahontas makes a medicine from milkweed. Tell the students to find out about other medicinal plants and their healing qualities. (Two excellent references for this activity are *Iroquois Medical Botany* by James W. Herrick, Syracuse University Press, 1995, and *If You Lived in Colonial Times* by Anne McGovern, Scholastic, 1964.)

=== Chapter 25 ===

| instigation | effrontery | consorted | bodkin | abhorred | apt | bombazine |
| mottled | acquittal | plaintive | vestry | parsonage | pagan | waver |

Activity: Marshal Dale set down a list of blue laws. Define and make a list of some blue laws. Explain why blue laws were first enacted. Find out what blue laws are in effect in your area.

=== Chapter 26 ===

| taffeta | coronet | surveyed | raspy | haughtily | peremptorily |

Activity: Brainstorm a list of words and phrases that describe how Tom might have felt when his cabin was destroyed. Assign the students to write a paragraph about Tom and how his cabin was ruined, incorporating as many of the brainstormed words and phrases as possible.

=== Chapter 27 ===

| prevailed | splendor | treason | retinue | somber | festooned | courtiers |

Activity: In the final chapter, Serena learns of Pocahontas' death. Pretend you are Serena and write an obituary for the local newspaper.

Vocabulary Development

Within the text of *The Serpent Never Sleeps,* you will find many words which can be explored in a variety of ways to help students expand their vocabularies. Here are some methods and activities for you to choose from and use with the class.

- Before the class begins reading *The Serpent Never Sleeps,* assign each student two or three words from the Colonial Word Banks on page 16. When they find their assigned words, have them note the page number and copy the sentence in which it appears.

- Provide each student or group with a copy of the Colonial Word Banks on page 16. As they read the novel, have them add words to the various categories.

- Write each vocabulary word on a separate index card or paper strip for use with pocket charts. Prepare additional cards or strips with articles (*a, an, the*) and prepositions (*of, into, after,* etc.). Students can use the cards or strips to build sentences.

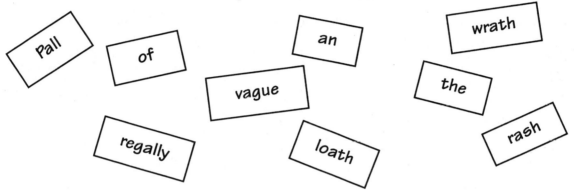

- On the chalkboard, write the name of a character from the story. Direct the students to look at the Descriptive Words list from page 16. Ask them to name words to describe that character; for example, Serena can be described as "lithesome" and "bonny." Pair students and let them complete descriptive lists of five other characters.

- Some words have more than one meaning. "Brook," for example, can mean "a small stream" but also "to tolerate." Copy the following list of words on the board: *stern, fathom, bluff, retainer, rash, poach, loom, consume.* Instruct students to write each word in two sentences to show the dual definitions. Have students draw accompanying pictures.

> *Brook: a small stream; to tolerate*
>
> *We crossed the babbling brook. I cannot brook further insults from you.*

- Let pairs of students create their own crossword puzzles, using some of the vocabulary words on page 16. Instruct them to include four words from each category in their puzzles. Provide the pairs with graph paper for easy construction. Check their accuracy before photocopying student-created puzzles for the class.

Colonial Word Banks

Use this page as a handy resource for creating spelling lists and various writing activities.

Ship Terms

bulwark	mainmast	sterncastle	galleon	hatches
stern	deck	gunnery room	fathoms	starboard
tall ships	longboat	gangplank	westerly winds	steering
crew	foredeck	pinnaces	bilge	rudder
sail	crow's nest	ballast	berth	bow

Ship Names

Deliverance	*Sea Venture*	*Neptune*	*Louisa Blessing*
Virginia	*Patience*	*Lion*	*Gates' Gift*

Geographical Terms

riverbank	swamps	isles	palisade	tall grass
mountains	forests	inlets	coral reef	salt meadows
bluff	tributaries	island	shoals	hillock
farmland	creeks	ocean	hillside	
stream	shores	bay	sea	

Native American Names

Pocahontas	Pamunkey River	Susquehanna	Chesapeake	Seanoc
Chief Powhatan	Algonquin	Masgawameke	Pastancie	Japazaws
Werowocomoco	Potomac River	Patowomek	Mattaponi	Opechancanough

Archaic Words

infernal	albeit	fortnight	preening	happenstance
clacker	victuals	quay	parlous	florid-faced
flusher	varlets	durance	ruse	vapors
galas	boon	rue	dipsey	ninny
masque	scullery	sugar-loaf	mnemosynon	bodkin
bonny	wench	hat	smitten	bombazine
doublet	thither	folly	twelvepence	festooned
fulsome	dithered	deem	whim	oakum

Descriptive Words

fearsome	arrogant	brackish	hapless	rash
contemptuous	sultry	withering	lofty	meager
stout	piebald	waning	faltering	boisterous
dejectedly	dour	meager	frolicsome	mottled
ponderous	eloquent	heedless	heedless	haughtily
lithesome	evasive	brazenly	heathenish	somber
bonny	pious	sprightly	regally	lighthearted

Places

Foxcroft	River Dane	London	Jamestown	Burmuda	Caribbean Sea
Potomac River	Plymouth	Calais	Bahamas	James River	Chesapeake Bay

Reading Response Journals

Assign a number of chapters for reading each day. Have students keep a Reading Response Journal. Some writing topics are provided for each block of chapters, beginning on this page and continuing on page 18.

Chapters 1-3

- What is your reaction to Countess Diana as she takes the serpent's ring from Serena? Explain how you would have handled the situation differently.

- Pretend you are either Serena or King James I and write a letter to a friend about your day's events. Include your impressions and predictions for what may happen next.

Chapters 4-6

- Serena was invited to the colonies by Captain John Smith, but she was also asked to work for the King's court. Which would you choose and why?

- Describe your feelings for Anthony Foxcroft. Explain your reaction to his accidental slaying of Carr's servant.

- Compare King James's views on smoking with those of medical experts today. Identify a current habit which shows possibilities of causing health problems in the future.

Chapters 7-9

- Compare Serena's feelings for Anthony with your own. Do you think she is making the right decision in following him? Why or why not?

- The serpent's ring has the power to protect Serena. Tell about a special good luck item of your own and what it enables you to do.

- Do you think names can "rule your life?" How do you feel about your name? If you could change your name, what would you call yourself?

Chapters 10-13

- The weary colonists were so thankful to finally touch land that they knelt to kiss the earth. Describe a time when you experienced a frightening situation and the actions you took once you were safe again.

- Find the Bahamas on a world map or globe. Judging from the islands' proximity to the equator, what climate would you expect to find there? What types of foods do you expect the settlers to find?

- Recall the scene in which Reverend Bucke gives a persuasive speech to the camp of colonists. What would you have said and done to motivate everyone to help?

- Review Governor Gate's decision not to take men with wives or children on the dangerous voyage to Jamestown. Explain how this situation would be handled in society today.

Chapters 13-15

- If you had to choose between Bermuda or the colonies, which would you choose and why?

- Presented with Serena's situation, would you favor the King and side with the loyalists or Francis Pearepoint and side with the conspirators? Justify your reasoning.

Reading Response Journals *(cont.)*

Chapters 13-15 *(cont.)*
- The new ship is to be named *Deliverance*. Tell why you think this is or is not a good name. Make a list of other possible names for the ship.

- Analyze Governor Gates' decision to take the life of Henry Paine. Why do you think he chose execution? What were some other options?

Chapters 16-19
- Describe your feelings as you are met by the starving, weak people of Jamestown.

- Imagine you are Powhatan standing on the shores of your land. Without warning, a ship carrying white settlers comes into your view. How would you describe what you have seen to the people in the village nearby?

- If you could bring Pocahontas to your home for one day, what is the one thing you would like to show her? Give reasons for your choice.

- Tell why you think Pocahontas would make a good friend.

Chapters 20-23
- Write ten phrases that describe your reaction to Marshal Dale and his "Laws of Blood."

- Characterize Emma Swinton. Compare her to a cartoon character or a movie character you have seen.

- Explain why you think Marshal Dale allowed Serena to join the search party for Pocahontas. What skills did Serena possess that would allow her to help in the negotiations?

- A new town, Henrico, was begun a few miles up the road. Was this a good idea? Defend your answer.

- Evaluate Captain Argall's and Captain Marshal Dale's reasons for finding Pocahontas. Explain why you agree or disagree with their actions.

Chapters 24-27
- John Rolfe had conflicting feelings about marrying Pocahontas. Name some of his fears. Were they justified?

- Compare the new settlement of Henrico to Jamestown. Choose which settlement you would prefer to live in. Explain your choice.

- Give your opinion of Reverend Whitaker's conversion of Pocahontas to Christianity. Were the Reverend's reasons justified? Explain.

- What do you think is the meaning of the book's title? How has your view changed since the beginning of the story?

Afterwards
- What do you think were the author's reasons for including the character Emma Swinton in the novel? Speculate what would have happened had Emma and Countess Diana sailed on the *Sea Venture* together.

- How might the story have been different if Anthony Foxcroft had lived?

- Do you think the serpent ring actually had protective powers? How do you think Serena would have fared if she hadn't worn the ring?

Character Webs

Character webs can produce a rich understanding of a story through analysis of the characters' emotions and feelings for one another.

Directions

1. Write the names of three related characters to head three columns on the board or overhead projector. For this example, the names Serena Lynn, Anthony Foxcroft, and King James will be used.

2. With the class, brainstorm how the characters feel toward one another. Write the responses in the appropriate columns.

Serena Lynn	Anthony Foxcroft	King James
is secretly in love with Anthony		thinks Anthony is moody

3. After the brainstorming session, draw a double triangle with one name at each corner, and with arrows to and from each name. Tell students that the directions of the arrows denote how one character feels toward another.

4. Write an appropriate response on each arrow. There can be more than one correct appropriate response for each line. Also, answers may change after reading subsequent chapters because the characters' relationships may also have changed.

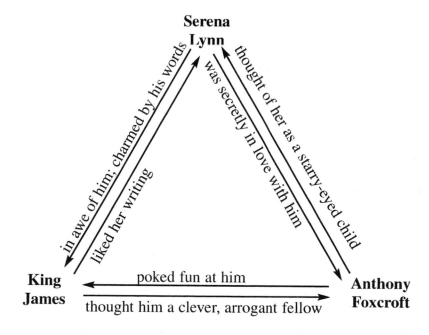

5. When students are comfortable with the process, divide them into small groups or pairs. Let them draw and complete a character web for any group of characters. Suggestions: Emma Swinton, Humility, and Serena Lynn; Captain Argall, Pocahontas, and Japazaws; John Smith, Pocahontas, and Serena Lynn; Tom Barlow, Serena, and Captain Argall.

Extensions

- Make a four-sided character web.

- Ask students to write a description of a character, based upon the information gathered.

- Make two character webs for the same three persons. Construct one web based on the characters at the beginning of the story; construct the second web based on the characters at some further point in the story.

Character Roster

Directions: As you encounter each new character in *The Serpent Never Sleeps,* enter his or her name on a space below. Fill in the chart with descriptive words and phrases about that character. Finally, describe that character's relationship to another character. An example has been done for you. (Use the back of this sheet if you need more room.)

Character	Descriptive Words/Phrases	Relationship
Edmund	keeper of Foxcroft's horses; loved danger and fishing	older brother of Serena Lynn

Pocahontas

Born about 1595, the daughter of Indian Chief Powhatan was affectionately called Pocahontas, which means "playful one." Pocahontas' relationship with the Jamestown colonists proved invaluable to the struggling community.

One autumn, reports came that white men were building a fort near the James River. Months later, news of a fierce battle came from Powhatan's brother, Opechancanough; some Indians had been taken prisoner. Captain John Smith promised to set the Indians free only if corn was brought to Jamestown. Powhatan agreed to the demands.

Weeks later, Opechancanough's men captured Captain Smith himself during another skirmish and took him to Powhatan at the village of Werowocomoco.

When Captain Smith was delivered by his captors, however, he was honored by the villagers. Opechancanough was furious! Two of his braves had been killed; the young chief demanded Smith's life in exchange. Yielding to his younger brother's demands, Chief Powhatan ordered Smith beaten to death. As the popular—and much-debated—story goes, guards raised their war clubs, but Pocahontas dashed forward and laid herself upon Smith to save him. A displeased Chief Powhatan gave in to his daughter's wishes and ordered the guards to drop their weapons.

Two days later, Smith was told that they were now friends. Indeed, Pocahontas brought food to the settlers when they were starving; in 1609, she warned Smith of an impending ambush. In turn, Smith taught the Indian princess English words.

When Smith was seriously injured in a gunpowder explosion in 1609, he returned to England before the severe winter and "the starving time" set in. Hoping to improve relations with the Powhatans, Captain Samuel Argall kidnapped Pocahontas and took her to Jamestown. There she was made to live at Reverend Alexander Whitaker's residence in Henrico, a town upriver from Jamestown. Pocahontas was taught how to read and given instruction in the English ways. When she was baptized into Christianity, she was given the name Rebecca.

In 1614, she married John Rolfe, a plantation owner. This marriage brought peace among the settlers and the Native Americans. One year after the birth of Thomas, the Rolfes' only child, the family traveled to England to promote the Jamestown colony.

Known to the English as Lady Rolfe, Pocahontas was presented at the court of King James I. Unfortunately, Pocahontas's health began to fail, mostly likely because Native Americans had little resistance to European diseases. After regaining some strength, Pocahontas and her family boarded a ship bound for America in 1617. As the ship was anchored in the Thames River, Pocahontas became weak and died at the age of 21. She was buried at Gravesend on March 21, 1617.

Pocahontas Crossword Puzzle

Directions: Write the words in the proper spaces on the crossword puzzle below. Answers to these clues can be found in the story on page 21.

Across

1. Smith was injured in a _____ explosion.
5. Powhatan's village
7. Pocahontas had no resistance to European _____.
10. Pocahontas' Christian name
11. daughter of Powhatan
13. John Rolfe owned a _____.
15. name of the Rolfes' child
17. town where captured Pocahontas was taken
18. meaning of Pocahontas

Down

2. Pocahontas' father
3. where Pocahontas visited Captain Smith
4. age at which Pocahontas died
6. Powhatan's brother
8. Pocahontas saved the life of this captain.
9. country toured by the Rolfe family
12. captain who captured Pocahontas
14. river where ship anchored in England
16. Pocahontas' English title

Teacher: Fold this answer section under before reproducing.

  Across: 1. gunpowder, 5. Werowocomoco, 7. diseases, 10. Rebecca,
        11. Pocahontas, 13. plantation, 15. Thomas, 17. Henrico, 18. playful one

  Down: 2. Powhatan, 3. Jamestown, 4. twenty-one, 6. Opechancanough, 8. John Smith,
        9. England, 12. Samuel Argall, 14. Thames, 16. Lady Rolfe

Word Problems

The *Serpent Never Sleeps* suggests several math activities. Either make and use an overhead transparency for whole-class discussion or pair or group the students to work together to find solutions. (**Note:** Be sure to cover the answers before displaying this page. If using the metric system, adjust measurements on this page accordingly.)

1. The men and women of the *Sea Venture* worked for hours pumping water from their leaking ship. In one day, 30 tons of water were removed from the ship's sterncastle. How much water was that? Use a calculator to determine how many pounds and how many gallons that would be.

   (Remember, one ton = 2000 lbs; one gallon = 8 lbs.)

2. Currently in America, each individual uses approximately 176 gallons of water per day. Pretending the ocean water was clean and drinkable, how many people would have been served by *Sea Venture's* unfortunate leak?

3. On page 23, Countess Diana is hosting a masque to raise funds for the Jamestown colony in Virginia. "Pitifully, fewer than a fifth of the one hundred ten who went out in 1607, just two years before, were still alive."

   Approximately how many of those colonists were still alive? What year was it?

4. During the six-month "starving time," fewer than sixty of the five hundred settlers had survived. What was the maximum number of settlers who died? What percentage of settlers was that?

5. One night while fishing for supper in the bay, Tom Barlow and Serena caught four tunny "...that must have weighed six hundred pounds between them." On average, what is the weight of each tunny? What fraction of a ton is six hundred pounds?

6. Shortly after the 150 settlers from Bermuda had made it to the colonies, 160 new people arrived at Jamestown. How many new settlers were there altogether? The 160 men, women, and children had sailed in on five ships. If they had been divided equally among the ships, how many people were aboard each ship?

7. Tom built a one-bedroom cabin in Henrico. It had a stone fireplace that was ten feet wide. How many inches is that?

8. The window in Tom's cabin was two feet high by two feet wide. What was the perimeter of the window? What was the area of the window?

Answers
1. 30 x 2,000 = 60,000 lbs; 60,000/8 = 7,500 gal.
2. 7,500/176 = 42 people
3. 110/5 = 22; 1607 + 2 = 1609
4. 500 - 59 = 441; 441/500 = .88 = 88%
5. 600/4 = 150; 600/2000 = 3/10 = 30%
6. 150 + 160 = 310; 160/5 = 32
7. 10 x 12 = 120 inches
8. P =2(l+w) P=2(2+2) P=8 ft.; A=s squared A=2 squared A=4 square feet

---

Science in the Colonies

―――――――――――――――――― **Solving the Water Problem** ――――――――――――――――――

When the colonists landed on Bermuda, they soon found themselves without safe drinking water, as the casks from the ship had run dry and the island had no streams. Building a solar water still could have solved the colonists' problem. (**Note:** Be sure to get permission to dig a hole on school property.)

Materials: shovel, sheet of plastic, rocks, small stones, plastic margarine cup or similar container

Procedure

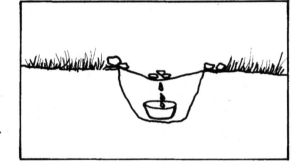

- Use the shovel to dig a cone-shaped hole.
- Place the cup in the middle of the hole.
- Spread the plastic sheet over the hole.
- Anchor the plastic in each corner with a rock.
- Place small stones in the center of the sheet.
- Check the container for water the next morning.

Explanation: During the day, the sun's rays warm the still, causing the temperature to rise. As temperatures cool in the evening, moisture condenses and collects on the plastic sheet. This moisture then falls into the container.

Note: The colonists did not have plastic sheets. What material could they have used instead?

―――――――――――――――――――――― **Drake's Raid** ――――――――――――――――――――――

Have a balloon race between a model of the *Drake* ship and a model of a Spanish ship.

Materials: patterns from page 25, scissors, two drinking straws cut to fit the back of the ships, two equal lengths of string, bookbinding or masking tape, two hot-dog shaped balloons, two chairs

Procedure

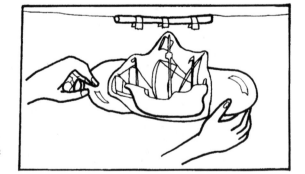

- Copy the ship patterns onto card stock and cut out.
- Thread one length of string through each straw.
- Tie each end of the string to a chair back.
- Move the chairs apart so that the string is taut.
- Attach three pieces of tape to each straw.
- Inflate the balloons and keep them pinched at the neck.
- Continue pinching as you attach the balloons to the straw and tape a ship to each balloon. (See diagram.)
- Slide both balloons to one end of the string.
- Release the balloons and watch as they glide along the string.

Explanation: The thrust provided by the released air in the balloon propels the balloon forward.

Ship Patterns

Directions: Copy the patterns below onto card stock and cut them out. Follow the directions for *Drake's* Raid on page 24.

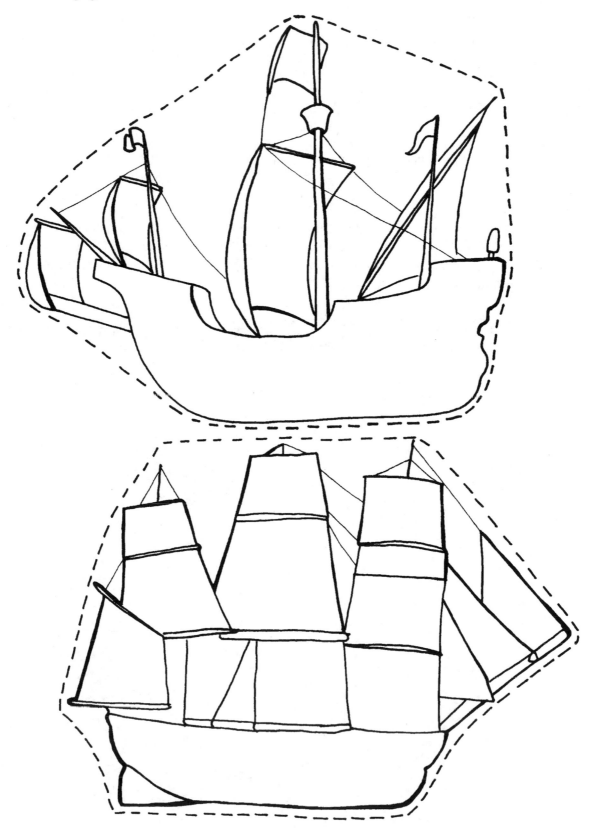

Researching Historical Figures

A number of historical figures are named in *The Serpent Never Sleeps*. Find out more about these individuals by completing one of the research projects presented below or on page 27. You may work individually or in groups.

King James I of England. As you read *The Serpent Never Sleeps*, copy the information about King James I from the novel. Research and find out more facts about King James I. Mark the information which appears both in your factual research and the novel.

Sir Walter Raleigh. On page 22 of the novel, Countess Diana compared her son with Sir Walter Raleigh. Research Sir Walter Raleigh and learn about his role in the founding of the colonies.

Sir Francis Drake. Countess Diana used a theme about Sir Francis Drake and his daring feat for her masque. Learn more about this explorer. When and where did he sail? What is his best known accomplishment?

Shakespeare. William Shakespeare was one of the guests in attendance at the masque. King James even quotes a passage from *MacBeth* on page 15 of *The Serpent Never Sleeps*: "Double, double, toil and trouble/Fire burn, and cauldron bubble." Find and read the rest of the passage from this play. Memorize this or another of Shakespeare's famous speeches.

Researching Historical Figures *(cont.)*

Pocahontas. Learn more about this Indian princess and her father, Powhatan. List story events about her from the novel; compare these to actual events in her life. Find out how she helped John Smith's fledgling colony and describe her relationship with him.

Captain John Smith. Captain Smith led a band of 140 men to settle Jamestown, Virginia, in May, 1607. Most of this group was composed of gentlemen intent on finding gold. They believed that there would be gems and gold littering the ground, there for the taking. What harsh realities awaited these gentlemen? What were the results of their failure to build shelter and hunt for food?

John Calvin. Some disgruntled members of the Church of England left the organization to form their own religion. Led by John Calvin, they became known as "Calvinists." Make a list of their beliefs and compare them to the beliefs of the Puritans.

Lord De La Warr. He described Jamestown as an unwholesome place; yet, he stayed and coaxed the colonists to work. Explain how he was able to convince the settlers that they all needed to help with building and planting. What do you think would have happened if he had not been so strict? Also, find out what state was named in his honor.

Artistic Endeavors

Both of the art projects on this page are directly related to *The Serpent Never Sleeps*. Read the presented passages before beginning either art activity.

Creating a Mnemosynon

Before the settlers left Bermuda and sailed on to the colonies, "Governor Gates set up in the admiral's garden a mnemosynon, a fair memorial of our experience on the island of Bermuda. It was made from the timber of our ruined ship in the figure of a cross and was fastened to a mighty cedar. In the center of the cross the governor placed a silver twelvepence, which bore the picture of King James."

Work in pairs to make a model of a mnemosynon.

Materials: tagboard or other heavy paper, pencil, scissors, twigs or sandpaper, glue, coins or aluminum foil, small seashells, and other appropriate small items

Procedure
- In pencil lightly draw the outline of a cross onto the tagboard. Cut out the shape.
- Cut twigs or sandpaper to fit the surface of the cross.
- Glue the twigs or sandpaper to the cross.
- Glue coins to the cross. To make your own coins, cut out tagboard circles and cover completely with aluminum foil.
- Glue some small seashells and other appropriate items to your mnemosynon.

Making Powhatan Masks

When Serena accompanied Governor Gates and his expedition to find Pocahontas, a fleet of canoes greeted them before they could land. The natives took them to their camp where "We sat for a time unattended, then three tall fellows painted half-black half-red, with white eyes and red strokes on their cheeks, came and danced. They wore robes made of blackish snakes stuffed with moss, the tails tied together in tassels."

Try your hand at making Powhatan masks. You may want to do some research to find out exactly how the natives painted their faces.

Materials: large Styrofoam ball, craft stick, white facial tissue, paper napkins or toilet paper, white household glue, water, pie pan, tempera paint (various colors), brushes

Procedure
- Mix glue with water to thin it and pour some into a pie pan. Crumple the tissue, napkins, or paper and dip it into the pan of glue.
- Mold the paper to the desired shape and attach it to Styrofoam ball. Push one end of a craft stick into the bottom of the ball and the other end into a clay base for support.
- Allow mask to dry overnight.
- Paint on features with the tempera paint.

Colonial Amusements

Although survival occupied most of everyone's time, the colonists did play games and have fun. Children's games included hide and seek (called "I Spy"), hopscotch, tag, and blindman's buff. Popular songs among the youngsters were "Here We Go 'Round the Mulberry Bush" and "London Bridge is Falling Down." In addition, there were separate boys' and girls' activities. Traditionally, boys played with tops and marbles, flew kites, climbed trees, and skated on ponds in winter. Girls, meanwhile, played with cornhusk dolls and learned to embroider. Older children enjoyed backgammon, checkers, dominoes, and cards. But all students can enjoy the following activities.

Indoor Games

Set up four centers in the room and have a different game at each one, such as backgammon, checkers, dominoes, and cards. Divide into four groups and determine a system for rotation from one center to another. Allow about ten to fifteen minutes at each center to sample some colonial fun.

Faux Samplers

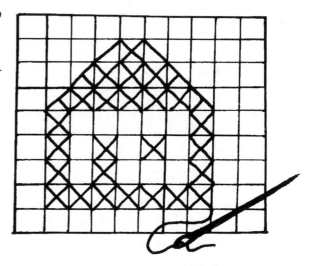

Learn to embroider. Enlist the help of those students who already know how or recruit parent volunteers. There is also an easy method you can use to create samplers, and it doesn't require a needle and thread. For this paper-and-pencil activity you will need graph paper and colored pencils. View and discuss some classic sampler designs, for example, the alphabet, animals, flowers, or brief sayings such as "A stitch in time saves nine." After determining a design, lightly sketch an outline of it onto the graph paper. With colored pencils, mark an "X" in each box until the design is complete. Color in the background, if desired, or add other features.

Blindman's Buff

Blindman's buff is a game still played by children today, although the rules have changed somewhat. Learn the original version. Everyone gathers into a circle and one person is chosen to be "buff." Blindfold "Buff" and place him or her in the center of the circle. Choose a second player to begin a conversation with Buff: "How many horses has your father got?" Buff answers, "Three." "What color are they?" Buff answers, "Black, white, and gray." "Turn about and turn about and catch whom you can." Buff spins around three times and tries to catch someone who then becomes buff. (Taken from *Colonial American Home Life* by John F. Warner, Franklin Watts, 1993.)

Colonial Foods

Indian Pudding

Early colonial settlers may have lacked some of the prepared foods they were used to in England, but they did not lack a natural food supply. The waters of the rivers and the ocean were teeming with fish, eels, clams, and oysters. Forests housed deer, pheasants, turkeys, and other game. Rich soil yielded a variety of fruits and vegetables. Of course, it was many years before the settlers learned how to farm and fish for themselves. In great part, the colonists had the Native Americans to thank because they shared their methods with the settlers. Most importantly, the Native Americans gave the Europeans the gift of corn, which came to be a staple in every colony. One sample of a popular corn dish is Indian Pudding.

Ingredients

- 3 $\frac{1}{2}$ cups (875 mL) water
- 1 teaspoon (5 mL) salt
- 1 $\frac{1}{4}$ cups (312 mL) yellow cornmeal
- butter or margarine
- nutmeg
- molasses

Utensils

- large, heavy saucepan
- $\frac{1}{4}$ cup (60 mL) measuring cup
- wood spoon

Directions: Pour the water and one teaspoon (5 mL) of salt into a large heavy saucepan. Bring the water to a boil and slowly add the cornmeal $\frac{1}{4}$ cup at a time, stirring constantly. Turn the heat down to a low setting and continue stirring until the mixture thickens. Spoon into bowls and top with butter, a sprinkle of nutmeg, and some molasses.

Currant Pound Cake

Pound cakes were so named because originally they were made with a pound of butter, a pound of sugar, a pound of flour, and numerous eggs. It took a strong arm to beat the batter by hand until the sugar was thoroughly blended in with the butter. The colonists used in their pound cakes currants dried right at home. The colonists also used brandy for plumping the currants and to give the cake added taste. You can make a tasty pound cake with a boxed cake mix.

Ingredients

- bundt cake mix
- any ingredients called for to make the mix
- $\frac{2}{3}$ cup (145 mL) raisins
- hot water
- cinnamon-sugar (1 tsp. /5 mL cinnamon to $\frac{1}{4}$ cup/63 mL sugar)

Utensils

- small bowl
- large bowl
- strainer
- wooden spoon
- small aluminum bread pans

Directions: Pour the raisins into the small bowl and add the hot water. Let the raisins soak for at least 30 minutes; drain. Prepare the bundt cake batter as directed on the package. Mix the batter by hand with the wood spoon. Make sure to get all the lumps out! Spoon the batter into greased bread pans. Sprinkle each loaf with cinnamon sugar. Bake as directed for small pans. When done, remove from pans and allow to cool. Slice the pound cakes and enjoy.

See the Bibliography for more books about colonial foods.

Meet Scott O'Dell

Scott O'Dell was born on May 23, 1898. Because O'Dell's father worked as an official with the Union Pacific Railroad, he and his family moved a lot. Mainly, though, they lived in California in what was then frontier country. Their homesite included a seaside village and an old gold-mining town southeast of Los Angeles on the Mexican border. Living in these various towns contributed to his choice of settings and characters throughout his novels.

Mr. O'Dell was educated at Long Beach Polytechnic High School and then went on to college. He then moved to Hollywood, where he taught a mail-order course in photoplay writing. From 1924 to 1925 he worked as a technical director for Paramount Motion Picture Studio. While attending the University of Rome he worked with Metro-Goldwyn-Mayer as a cameraman on the set of the original "Ben Hur." Upon returning to Los Angeles, O'Dell worked as a book editor and a book columnist for two local newspapers.

Throughout his college years he maintained an interest in fiction writing, but it wasn't until 1934 that his first novel was published, entitled *Woman of Spain: A Story of Old California*. In 1960, his first novel for young children was published—*Island of the Blue Dolphins* which garnered nine awards, including a Newbery Medal. Three subsequent novels—*The King's Fifth, The Black Pearl,* and *Sing Down the Moon*—were named Newbery Honor Books. O'Dell also received the prestigious Hans Christian Andersen medal for his body of work.

Mr. O'Dell's love for history shows in the many historical novels he has written. He chose these generally because he felt that children need to know and understand the past. On this issue he comments:

> *"For children, who believe that nothing much has happened before they appeared and that what little of the past they do perceive has any possible bearing upon their lives, the historical novel can be an entertaining corrective, a signpost between the fixed, always relevant, past and the changing present."*

Altogether, Scott O'Dell wrote 25 books for young people, the last, *My Name Is Not Angelica*, in 1989. That was the same year that he died of cancer. He was 91 years old.

Activities

- If you could have met Scott O'Dell, what three questions would you have asked him about his work?

- Make a list of other books that O'Dell penned (use the card catalog in your library to assist you). Choose one and read it.

- Read any two books written by Scott O'Dell. Compare them on the following points: *setting, theme, plot,* and *point of view.*

*(Quotations from **Something About the Author**. Ed. Anne Commire. Gale Research Company)*

The Witch of Blackbird Pond

by Elizabeth George Speare

Summary

The Witch of Blackbird Pond is an adventure, romance, and history novel, all wrapped in one. The heroine of this tale is Katherine Tyler—"Kit"—an impulsive, independent, 16 year old. Her grandfather has just died, and she leaves her home on Barbados to live with her aunt and uncle in Connecticut, where things are so much different. Endless household chores fill her days, and she must learn new ways. Reluctantly, Kit trades her silk dresses for plain, unadorned calico that is better suited to her new lifestyle. But when lonely Kit befriends a suspected witch, the Puritan village turns against her. Handsome Nat Eaton, whom she met on the *Dolphin*, comes to her rescue.

This outline is a suggested plan for using the various activities that are presented in this book. You should adapt these ideas to fit your own classroom situation and the ability level of your students.

Sample Plan

Lesson 1
- Define "witch." (page 33)
- Locate England, Barbados, and Connecticut. (page 33)
- Research Barbados; complete the mapping activity. (page 51)
- Discuss prejudice. (page 33)
- Read Chapter 1.
- Read and discuss the poem "Pilgrims and Puritans." (page 33)
- Research topic number one. (page 41)

Lesson 2
- Read Chapters 2-4.
- Create math word problems. (page 35)
- Make soap. (page 43)
- Assign appropriate research topics. (page 41)

Lesson 3
- Read Chapters 5-7.
- Learn about Pilgrim manners. (page 41)
- Make apple tarts. (page 43)
- Do the art project: Dyeing and Weaving. (page 44)
- Continue assigning research topics. (page 41)

Lesson 4
- Read Chapters 8-10.
- Rewrite good manners passage. (page 36)
- Create word problems. (page 36)
- Write a conversation between Kit and William. (page 37)
- Continue research topics. (page 41)

Lesson 5
- Read Chapters 11-12.
- Make a model of Kit's hornbook. (pages 45-46)
- Do the activities for chapters. (page 37)
- Research Anne Bradstreet; write a brief biography. (page 42)
- Continue assigning research topics. (page 42)

Lesson 6
- Read Chapters 13-15.
- Do the activities for chapters. (pages 37-38)
- Plan a husking bee and competition. (page 46)
- Make succotash. (page 46)
- Create "fall leaves." (page 47)
- Assign appropriate research topics. (page 42)

Lesson 7
- Read Chapters 15-17.
- Do the activities for chapters. (pages 37-38)
- Discuss views on taxation. (page 38)
- Draw jack-o-lanterns. (page 38)
- Write a cinquain. (page 40).
- Assign appropriate research topics. (page 43)

Lesson 8
- Read Chapters 18-21.
- Do the activities for chapters. (page 39)
- Grow stalactites. (page 47)
- Write a rebus story. (page 48)
- Make pussywillows. (page 39)
- Assign appropriate research topics. (page 42)
- Learn about Elizabeth George Speare. (page 52)

Overview of Activities

SETTING THE STAGE

1. **Define the word "witch".** Write the word "witch" on the chalkboard. Ask the students to define the term; record their responses. Discuss the special powers witches are purported to possess, how it can be determined whether a person is a witch, and what students know about the witch hunts in the early colonial days.

2. **Mapping.** Display a wall map that shows Europe and North America. Have students locate key places relevant to *The Witch of Blackbird Pond*: England, Barbados, and Connecticut.

3. **Prejudice.** Ask students whether they can recall a time when they formed a wrong opinion of a person before actually knowing that individual. What caused them to form their opinion—the person's looks? Something the person said or did? Direct students to think about how they unfairly treated that person, and what happened to improve the situation.

ENJOYING THE BOOK

1. **Reading the Pages.** Assign a number of chapters to read for each lesson. Suggested amounts are specified in the sample plan on page 32.

2. **Think and Do Activities.** Reinforce each chapter's reading with the corresponding activities on pages 35-39. These pages provide a discussion topic and an activity to accompany each chapter.

3. **Vocabulary Ideas.** The activities on pages 35-39 also include a list of suggested vocabulary words for each chapter.

4. **Poetry and Writing.** Activities to strengthen students' writing skills include point of view and cinquains poetry on page 40.

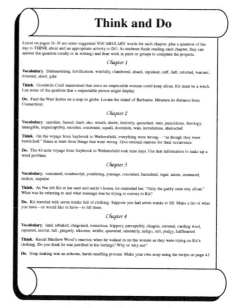

5. **Research Topics.** Assign pairs or groups to find out more about the topics presented on pages 41-42. Students are asked to make a Venn diagram, write a biography, draw and label a ship, and read poetry, for example.

6. **Research.** In the opening scenes of the book, we meet Kit Tyler, who is traveling from her Barbados home to Wethersfield, Connecticut. Learn about the small island of Barbados with the paired mapping activity on page 51.

7. **Reading Poetry.** Read the poem "Pilgrims and Puritans" by Rosemary and Stephen Vincent Benét (from *A Book of Americans*, Henry Holt, 1986). Discuss the similarities of Puritan influences as they relate to Kit Tyler. Examine Puritan influences which are still present in life today.

Overview of Activities *(cont.)*

ENJOYING THE BOOK *(cont.)*

8. **Colonial Sampler.** Experience colonial life with any of the arts, crafts, and cooking projects on pages 43-47. Correlate the activities to the appropriate chapters wherever possible. Projects to choose from include making soap, cooking succotash, making quills and bark to write on, and growing stalactites (crystals).

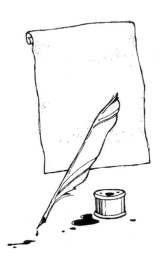

9. **Learning Is Fun.** Compare schooling conditions of the colonial era with those today. Students can experience some typical methods used by teachers of that time. See these ideas on page 48.

10. **Colonial Ship.** Label a typical ship from the colonial era. See page 49 for a prepared worksheet.

11. **Quotes.** Test students' knowledge about characters with the group project on page 50.

EXTENDING THE BOOK

1. **Choosing Eras.** With the class, make a list of advantages and disadvantages of life during the colonial era. Ask students to evaluate in which era they would prefer to live, the late 1600s or the present. Have the students justify their choices. Make a graph of their choices.

2. **Museums.** If possible, visit a living history museum where students can see colonial life in action. Jamestown Settlement in Williamsburg, Virginia, is probably the most authentic and best known. This museum contains a full-scale replica of the original Jamestown settlement and three original ships that carried the first settlers there. Period activities are performed by people in historic attire. Check in your area for living museums or invite a guest historian to your classroom to demonstrate spinning or weaving, for example.

3. **Comparisons.** Compare a character from *The Serpent Never Sleeps* to a character from *The Witch of Blackbird Pond*. Assign two different characters to each group of students. Direct them to construct a Venn diagram of the likenesses and differences. Characters to compare include Emma Swinton and Goodwife Cruff, Serena Lynn and Kit Tyler, Tom Barlow and Nat Eaton.

4. **Meet the Author.** Meet author Elizabeth George Speare. Find out what other books she has written. Complete any of the follow-up activities on page 52.

5. **A Question of Slavery.** Investigate further the slave trade as it developed in the colonies. Find out in which colonies the practice was most prevalent and learn why it was instituted.

6. **Original Colonies.** Study the history of the original 13 colonies with the mini-unit on pages 53-63.

Think and Do

Listed on pages 36-39 are some suggested VOCABULARY words for each chapter, plus a question of the day to THINK about and an appropriate activity to DO. As students finish reading each chapter, they can answer the question (orally or in writing) and then work in pairs or groups to complete the projects.

Chapter 1

Vocabulary. disheartening, fortification, wistfully, clambered, aback, repulsed, cuff, daft, retorted, warrant, diverted, aloof, gale

Think. Goodwife Cruff maintained that since no respectable woman could keep afloat, Kit must be a witch. List some of the qualities that a respectable person might display.

Do. Find the West Indies on a map or globe. Locate the island of Barbados. Measure its distance from Connecticut.

Chapter 2

Vocabulary. tantalize, fumed, daub, eke, wraith, shrew, furtively, quenched, vent, punctilious, theology, intangible, imperceptibly, recoiled, constraint, squall, dominion, wan, incredulous, abstracted

Think. On the voyage from Saybrook to Wethersfield, everything went wrong— "as though they were bewitched." Name at least three things that went wrong. Give rational reasons for their occurrence.

Do. The 43-mile voyage from Saybrook to Wethersfield took nine days. Use that information to make up a word problem.

Chapter 3

Vocabulary. restrained, nondescript, pondering, passage, conceded, burnished, regal, intent, measured, reckon, impulse

Think. As Nat left Kit at her aunt and uncle's house, he reminded her, "Only the guilty ones stay afloat." What was he referring to and what message was he trying to convey to Kit?

Do. Kit traveled with seven trunks full of clothing. Suppose you had seven trunks to fill. Make a list of what you have—or would like to have—to fill them.

Chapter 4

Vocabulary. fend, rebuked, chagrined, tremulous, frippery, perceptibly, chagrin, retorted, carding wool, repented, mortal, tuft, gingerly, irksome, writhe, quavered, unseemly, indigo, tuft, pudgy, halfhearted

Think. Recall Matthew Wood's reaction when he walked in on the women as they were trying on Kit's clothing. Do you think he was justified in his feelings? Why or why not?

Do. Soap making was an arduous, harsh-smelling process. Make your own soap using the recipe on page 43.

Think and Do *(cont.)*

Chapter 5

Vocabulary. threshold, surveyed, affront, mock, popish, baffled, placating, auspiciously, repress, tactlessness, pillory, undulated, brandishing, chinks, pauper, venomous, staidness, demurely, nonplussed

Think. Kit's uncle disapproved of her Sunday clothes. Name at least three possible solutions that could solve this problem. Choose which solution you think would be best; defend your answer.

Do. Fold a sheet of drawing paper in half. On one side draw a picture of Kit's Sunday dress; on the other side draw a picture of Judith's dress.

Chapter 6

Vocabulary. warrant, allegiance, coddle, cadence, meddle, terse, petition, placid, inexorably, appraisal

Think. "And bless our sister in her weakness and affliction." Do you think these words apply to Mercy? Defend your answer.

Do. Reverend Bulkeley enjoyed and praised Rachel's tarts. Make apple tarts with the recipe on page 43.

Chapter 7

Vocabulary. cordially, lapse, twanged, implacable, reckoning, veritable, airily, substantial, provoking, charter

Think. Recall the heated political debate between Matthew and William. Construct a chart comparing their views.

Do: Wool shearing brought new chores—dyeing and weaving. Try a dyeing and weaving project on page 44.

Chapter 8

Vocabulary. menial, encroaching, dame school, dubiously, rankled, solitary, vigorously, triumph, communion

Think. When a calico dress is made for Kit, her relationship with Judith seems to improve. Explain why.

Do. Every child paid fourpence per week to attend dame school. Create some math word problems about how many children would attend, for how long, and how much money Kit and Mercy would earn.

Chapter 9

Vocabulary. unison, allotted, conjured, sober, precarious, ingenious, composure, ruffled, indulgence, enthralled, parable, raiment, obstreperous, priggish, hapless, cordially, bedlam, decorum, ravenous, tangibly

Think. Find and reread the words the children said in unison on page 82 of the novel. Why do you think teachers used chanting and rhyming in their lessons? Do these methods help you learn?

Do. Rewrite it for modern times. Locate a passage from Eleazar Moody's *A School of Good Manners* (1772).

Think and Do *(cont.)*

Chapter 10

Vocabulary. malicious, impassive, bewitched, distressed, torment, literally, tart, toady, perched, sparse, fervent, bide, sacraments, unorthodox, diligently, intense, contradictory, mocking, incredulously, vagueness

Think. No one will have anything to do with Hannah Tupper. How is she different from other townspeople? Are their fears justified?

Do. Write a conversation Kit might have with William Ashby as she explains to him why Hannah is neither harmful nor evil.

Chapter 11

Vocabulary: serenely, pious, docilely, cherished, filigree, blanched, resolutely, morsel, wary, qualms, adroit, discern, resin, hastily, reverent, rebel, heresy

Think. When Kit realizes that Mercy loves John Holbrook, she thinks it is both right and impossible. What predictions do you make for romance between these two characters?

Do. Reread the description of Kit's hornbook on pages 114-115 of the novel. Make a model of her hornbook, using the directions on page 46 of this book.

Chapter 12

Vocabulary. tallow, becalmed, latitude, cross-staff, retain, nonchalant, spry, detained, consternation, apprehension, restrained, morosely

Think. When Nat was a child, he wanted to bring back a bird from Jamaica, but his father talked him out of it. Explain why Kit reminded him of that bird.

Do. Write a list of the chores that were waiting for Kit in mid-August. Compare those to any household chores you might have.

Chapter 13

Vocabulary. husking bee, wresting, blithely, merriment, crimson, ventured, imposing, propitious, drudgery, foreboding, mite, contrite, lingered, incredulous, provocatively, rebuked, lustrous, unwanted, perplexed, resolutely, forfeit, radiance, indulgently, constraint, irrelevantly

Think. Judith mistakenly thinks John has come to ask her father for her hand in marriage. Only Kit knows the truth. Why do you think Kit remained silent? Why didn't John explain the miscommunication?

Do. Husk some corn. Scrape the kernels off with a knife and make succotash (see a sample recipe on page 46).

Think and Do *(cont.)*

Chapter 14

Vocabulary. buoyant, defiant, to and fro, expectancy, bustling, hoity-toity, surge, fretted, eavesdropped, scouring, indifferent

Think. Explain Nat's reserved greeting of Kit and his biting remarks to her. Why do you think he spoke to her that way? What do you think his real feelings were?

Do. "The oaks along the roadway glowed yellow and bronze. The fields stretched like a carpet of jewels, emerald and topaz and garnet." Draw a picture of this fall scene or complete the "Fall Leaves" art project on page 47.

Chapter 15

Vocabulary. commonwealth, defy, faltered, seething, emerged, aspect, scoffed, condescending, mishap, chagrined, brusquely, cavalier, resignation, raucous, elated, insubordination, dictated, dispute, grenadier

Think. What were Kit's views and feelings about Uncle Matthew? How did this change when she learned about his small act of insubordination?

Do. Work in pairs, with one student playing Governor Andros and the other playing Matthew Wood in a presentation of opposing views on taxation.

Chapter 16

Vocabulary. roistering, mortified, blasphemy, ordeal, repentance, unchastened, impelled, banished, reconcile, treatise, unperturbed, ruefully, tryst, retribution, wistfully, poignant, reproachful

Think. Judith and Mercy have different reactions to the news that John enlisted in the militia. What does Mercy understand that Judith does not?

Do. Draw and design a different scary jack-o-lantern to place in each of the sixteen windows of William Ashby's house.

Chapter 17

Vocabulary. moping, delirious, malady, vitality, vigil, remote, rouse, rasp, poultice, consternation, consorting, infidel, slander, receded, frantic, serenity, tantalizingly, plague, docile, obstinate, sodden

Think. When an illness befalls the settlement, a group of men decides that it must be the fault of the witch, Hannah. What is their reasoning?

Do. Kit has a choice between going with Nat to his grandmother's or staying behind to help with Mercy. What would have been your choice? Explain.

Think and Do *(cont.)*

Chapter 18

Vocabulary. consented, haggard, contempt, scornful, cunning, jibed, laxness, quavered, blanched, ventured, conviction, sustained, flouting, inveigled, magistrate, champion, vengeance

Think. What evidence did the townspeople have that Hannah was a witch? What evidence did they have against Kit? Be able to explain each of the charges.

Do. Kit hopes that William will come to her rescue, but only Aunt Rachel visits her where she is detained. Predict the outcome of Kit's forthcoming trial.

Chapter 19

Vocabulary. dubious, cronies, anguish, sundry, instigation, preternatural, infer, countenance, enchantments, mockery, tainted, pandemonium, trifle, deliberative, bluster, frenzy, clarity, sustaining, vouch, venomous, remit, prompted, recounted, testimony, deceitful, vented, interceded

Think. What were some of the complaints against Kit? Why did Matthew Wood protest the mockery? Was he correct in doing so?

Do. Prudence used the copybook to practice writing her name. Staple a number of lined writing pages together to make your own copybook. Practice writing a passage from the book in your neatest hand.

Chapter 20

Vocabulary. resented, detachment, perforce, levelly, conceded, baffled, meager, surreptitiously, concocting, bleak, veranda, vivid, resolve, inescapable, amending, biding, resolve, abate, perceptibly

Think. As William is explaining his actions to Kit, he tells her, "We're judged by the company we keep." What did he mean by this statement? Do you think it is true or false? Defend your answer.

Do. Sometimes Kit would talk to Mercy about Barbados. Once, she told her about an underwater cave in which colored icicles hung from the ceiling. Explore the topic of stalactites and grow some by using the directions on page 47.

Chapter 21

Vocabulary. dowries, hoarding, cherished, illusions, governess, ketch, arc, ordeal, beckoning, eluded, queried, chipper, surge, unpremeditated

Think. While Kit was thinking about leaving Wethersfield, she remembered something that Hannah had once told her: "There is no escape if love is not there." Explain what this quote means to you.

Do. "A low bush nearby had blossomed in tiny gray balls." Make pussywillows. Paint long brown stems on white paper. Tear off sections of cotton puffs and roll them into oval shapes. Glue the ovals at intervals along the stems.

Poetry and Writing

Foster your creativity with any of the poetry and writing ideas on this page. Use new vocabulary words wherever possible.

Cinquains

Write cinquains, following directions for each line. An example follows.

Subject (noun)	**Kit**
2 adjectives describing the subject	headstrong, impetuous
3 action verbs ending in -ing	loving, longing, hoping
phrase to describe the subject	for pristine days in Barbados
synonym for the subject	Katherine Tyler

Chant

Schoolmistresses used chants to help their young charges remember lessons such as, "Good children must/Fear God all day/Parents obey/No false thing say/By no sin stray." Make up your own chants for learning facts such as multiplication tables or even rules of geometry.

Point of View

Write about a specific event from the point of view of several characters. For example, Nat informs Kit that he has 16 diamond-paned windows for William Ashby's new house. Write a diary entry explaining how Nat, Kit, and William each felt about the situation.

What If?

With your class, compose possible "What if?" questions. For example, what if Kit had married William? What if John had died while he was enlisted? What if Kit had been found guilty of witchcraft? List the questions on the board and discuss possible answers to the questions.

Qualities

Brainstorm with the class to make a list of Kit's good and not-so-good qualities. Explore how her good qualities helped her out and how her not-so-good qualities got her into trouble. Then either write about a time when Kit's good qualities were helpful to her or about a time when Kit's poorer qualities caused her a problem.

Research Topics

The text of *The Witch of Blackbird Pond* suggests a number of different topics to research and learn more about. Both here and on page 42, you will find a research project for each chapter. Let students choose from the projects or assign a project to pairs or groups.

- Kit wondered, "Which one of those queer little boxlike houses did they call home?" Draw a typical seventeenth century saltbox home. Find out why that type of architecture was so popular in that part of the country. Also, find out what a colonial-style building looked like; draw a picture of a typical colonial style home.

- Slaves from Barbados were on board the *Dolphin,* but Kit was unaware of them. Research the slave trade and write a one-page report about the origins of the slaves and the industries in which they were used. Read a story about the life of a slave. Some possible resources are *Amos Fortune: Free Man* by Elizabeth Yates (Dutton, 1950) and *Tituba of Salem Village* by Ann Petry (Harper & Row, 1964).

- Royalists supported King James II, but when the king tried to take charge in the colonies by sending Sir Edmund Andros to New England, some colonists became upset. Find out more about King James II, his beliefs about the monarchy, and his religious views. Write a brief biography.

- Colonists had to make the soap with which they washed. Since it was such a difficult task, soap was made only once or twice a year. Two basic ingredients of soap were animal fat and lye. Learn how lye soap was made; make a flow chart showing the steps in the process. Two excellent resources for this project are *Colonial American Home Life* by John F. Warner, Franklin Watts, 1993, and *Kids' America* by Stephen Caney, (Workman Publishing, 1978).

- Sometimes families traveled great distances to attend church on the Sabbath and could not go home between services. Out of necessity, Sabbath houses were established. Draw a picture of a typical Sabbath house. Write a story explaining how a family might spend their Sabbath there.

- Pewterware, cups, spoons, and trenchers were not washed after meals because there was no running water. Explain how the dishes were cleaned. A wonderful resource for this project is the book *Eating the Plates: A Pilgrim Book of Food and Manners* by Lucille Recht Penner (Macmillan, 1991).

- Kit faced endless chores. Dyeing and weaving wool, drawing water, and hoeing and weeding vegetables were among them. Find out and make a list of some of the daily chores that even young children were expected to do.

- Compare the religious convictions of Puritans with those views held by Quakers. Draw a Venn diagram to show the likenesses and differences between the two religions.

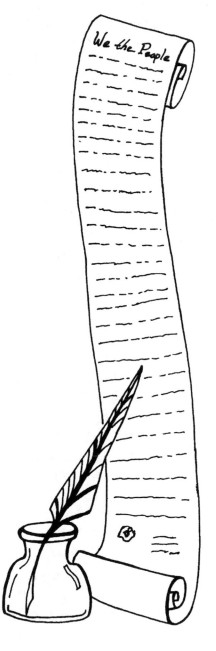

Research Topics *(cont.)*

- Anne Bradstreet was the wife of the governor of Massachusetts. She is also an important figure in the literary world. Write a brief biography of her and her role in history. Read some of her poetry.

- Shakespeare wrote *The Tempest* after he read about the storm that wrecked the *Sea Venture* off the coast of Bermuda. Find out more about the play; describe the characters Miranda and Prospero. Learn some facts about Shakespeare's life by reading *Lives of the Writers* by Kathleen Krull (Harcourt Brace & Company, 1994).

- Colonists organized "bees" throughout the year to harvest corn, make a quilt, build a home, or gather maple syrup. Research and explain the importance and purpose of these gatherings, who participated, and what was done at each. Make a chart to show the different types of bees.

- Colonial men were in charge of political decisions; women had no say in such matters. How does this compare with politics today in America? Find out about some countries where women are not yet allowed to participate in politics.

- A plague devastated London, England, in the 1660s. When a fire began in a bakery and destroyed most of the city's old wood houses, the plague germs were also gone. Research to find out why this occurred, how plague is spread, what bubonic plague is, and learn about any recent outbreaks of plague around the world.

- When the United States Constitution was written, ten amendments which guarantee citizens' rights were promptly added. Find out which Constitutional amendment makes provisions against false imprisonment. What does it mean to you?

- Kit was fortunate that she was found innocent of witchcraft. Others during that period were not so lucky. Learn what tests were given to determine whether a man or a woman was a witch and how witches were tried. Draw a poster which explains how to tell whether someone is a witch or make a poster containing advice on protection against witches.

- Snow was something new to Kit as she had never seen it at her Barbados home. Learn about the climate of Barbados and compare it to the climate of New England. Draw a picture to show the seasonal changes in New England; draw another picture to show the seasonal changes in Barbados.

- In Chapter 21, Nat ties up a brand new ketch at Wethersfield landing. It is ". . . fresh-painted, with clean white canvas and not a barnacle on its hull." Find out more about ships of the colonial era. Draw a picture of a typical colonial ship and label its parts (see page 49 for a prepared worksheet). Some excellent resources are *A Goodly Ship: The Building of the Susan Constant* by Peter H. Spectre and David Larkin (Houghton Mifflin, 1992) and *Inside Story: A 16th Century Galleon* by Richard Humble (Peter Bendrick Books, 1995).

A Colonial Sampler

On pages 43-47 are a number of arts, crafts, and cooking experiences that typify life in colonial times. You may either pick and choose or correlate the activities to specific chapters.

Recipe for Soap (Chapter 4)

Soap making was a time-consuming task. First, animal fat had to be gathered; then, lye had to be made by pouring boiling water over a mixture of wood ashes and straw for a week or more. Then it was time to cook the ingredients, which had to be stirred constantly. The resulting lye soap was quite harsh and did not lather readily like modern soaps. Students can get an idea of the soap making process, using the recipe below.

Ingredients: baking soda, salad oil, water

Utensils: 1/2-cup measuring cup, glass or enamel saucepan (cannot be metal), wood or plastic spoon (cannot be metal), stove top or hot plate, glass or clear plastic jars with lids, teaspoon

Directions: Measure and pour 1/2 cup (125 mL) of baking soda, salad oil, and water into the pan. Mix and then simmer over low setting; stir occasionally. The mixture will thicken suddenly as the water evaporates. Continue to heat it for a few more minutes before letting it cool. Drop a teaspoon (5 mL) of the mixture into each jar and add some hot water. Attach the lid and shake the jar; watch the suds appear.

Apple Tarts (Chapter 6)

After Reverend Bulkeley dines with Matthew Woods and his family, he compliments Rachel on her cooking: "I warrant there's not a housewife in the colonies can duplicate your apple tarts." You may not be able to, either, but you can enjoy this tasty—and easy—apple tart.

Ingredients: 3-inch (7.5 cm) ready-made graham cracker shells, jars of applesauce, cinnamon, strawberry preserves, prepared whipped cream

Utensils: mixing bowl, 2 spoons

Directions: Mix 1 teaspoon (5 mL) cinnamon with each cup (250 mL) of applesauce. Spoon applesauce into each tart shell. Top with a spoonful of strawberry preserves and a dollop of whipped cream.

A Colonial Sampler *(cont.)*

Dyeing and Weaving (Chapter 7)

With the help of Native Americans and through their own experimentation, the colonists learned how to use plants for dyes. After some time, the colonists were able to make enough indigo dye to export some to England.

Use the directions below to make your own natural dye.

Materials: scissors, 1 pound (500 g) of dry outer skins from brown onions, two cooking pots, water, stove top or hot plate, strainer, cotton cloth, such as diapers, handkerchiefs, sheets, or old T-shirts

Directions: Using scissors, cut the onion skins into small pieces. Place them in a pot, cover them with water, and soak overnight. Cook the onion-water mixture over medium heat for an hour. Strain the dyed water into another pot; allow to cool.

Cut the cloth into 8" x 8" (20 cm x 20 cm) squares and place them into the dyed water; add enough water to cover the cloth. Place the pan back onto the burner and simmer ten or fifteen minutes. Remove the cloth and rinse in cool water; dry it away from sunlight. Experiment with other natural dyes—e.g., dandelion leaves produce yellow-green dye, and red hollyhocks produce pink.

Weaving (Chapter 7)

Colonists had to make their own cloth. First, they harvested plants such as flax. After the fibers were taken from the plant and processed, they were spun into thread on a spinning wheel. This thread was then woven into cloth for shirts, blouses, and even table napkins.

While it is not likely that you could duplicate this process in the classroom, students can have fun with this weaving experience.

Materials: plastic berry baskets, craft yarn and knitting yarn in a variety of colors, ribbon, scissors

Directions: Tie a length of ribbon yarn to the bottom right hand corner of one of the faces of the box. Weave the ribbon over and under through the plastic squares until you get all the way around the box once; tie it off. With another length of ribbon or yarn make another row in the same manner. Push the rows together as they are completed.

A Colonial Sampler *(cont.)*

Making Quills (Chapter 9)

Ballpoint pens were unheard of in Colonial America. Instead, people used goose quill pens dipped in homemade ink. Paper was expensive and scarce so students had to use birch bark. Re-create colonial writing with the two projects below.

Materials: wing feather from a goose, turkey, seagull, or crow; sharp knife; pencil; liquid ink (available at office or art supply stores)

Directions: Follow these steps to make your own quill pen.

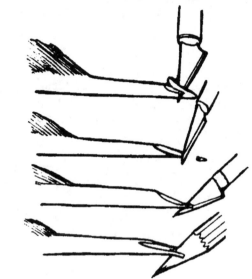

1. With the knife, make an angled cut on the underside of the wing tip.
2. Cut the tip square.
3. Slit the tip just a little.
4. Press open with a pencil.

Making Bark (Chapter 9)

Materials: brown paper shopping bags, scissors, brown tempera paint, paint brushes

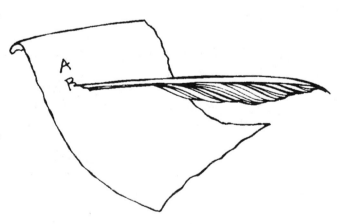

Directions: With scissors, cut open the shopping bags. By hand, tear sheets with jagged edges to resemble bark. Crumple and then smooth out the sheets. Write on the "bark" with quill and ink, leaving a 1" (2.54 cm) margin around all edges. Lightly brush brown tempera paint around the edges of the paper.

A Colonial Sampler *(cont.)*

Hornbooks (Chapter 9)

Colonial children received little formal education. What lessons they did receive were usually from the Bible; hornbooks were the only other teaching aid. A hornbook consisted of a page of writing that was fastened to a wooden frame. The writing was covered with a translucent sheet of animal horn. Make a hornbook with modern materials.

Materials: scissors, cardboard face from a cereal box, red construction paper, white glue, black calligraphy marking pen (available in art, school, or office supply stores), tongue depressor, aluminum foil, clear tape, acetate, stapler

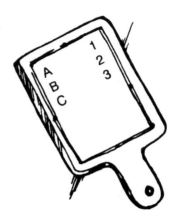

Directions: Cut out both large sides of cereal boxes; each student will need both sections. Round off the edges of the cardboard. Cut sheets of red construction paper to fit the cardboard. Glue one piece of construction paper to each piece of cardboard; allow to dry. With the calligraphy pen, write the letters of the alphabet and the numerals from 0 to 9 on one page and some proverbs or sayings on the other side. Place the cardboard pieces back to back and staple along the edges, leaving a space at the bottom for the tongue depressor. Staple the tongue depressor between the two pieces of cardboard. Cover the handle and outer edges of the cardboard with aluminum foil. Cover each face with a piece of acetate cut to the shape of the hornbook; staple the acetate to the top of each page.

Succotash (Chapter 13)

Because some jobs were too big for just one family to get done, neighborhood work parties or "bees" were held. During a husking bee everyone helped shuck the corn. Competitions were conducted to see who could husk the most corn in a given period of time. Afterwards, there might be music, dancing, or games. Plan a classroom husking bee. Use the corn to make a typical colonial corn dish—succotash; an easy recipe follows.

Ingredients: water; 4 ears of fresh corn; 1 ten-ounce (300 g) box of frozen lima beans (or 1½ cups (375 mL) fresh beans, if available; salt and pepper; one tablespoon (15 mL) of butter or margarine

Utensils: knives, saucepan, spoon, stove top or hot plate

Directions: With a knife, scrape the kernels from the corn cobs. Put the kernels and lima beans in the saucepan; add enough water to cover the vegetables. Cook over medium heat for about ten to fifteen minutes until the vegetables are heated through. Drain the water. Mix the vegetables with the butter and a sprinkling of salt and pepper to taste.

A Colonial Sampler *(cont.)*

Fall Leaves (Chapter 14)

Kit was amazed at the sight of the colorful oak and maple leaves. Anyone who has ever witnessed this transformation can attest to the beauty of a New England autumn. Make your own autumn leaves with the art project below.

Materials: paper and pencil, colored art tissue, scissors, white glue, water, plastic margarine cups, paint-brushes, wax paper, newspaper, black fine-line marking pen or black tempera paint

Directions: In the margarine cups, mix the glue with water; set aside. Cover the work surface with newspaper; top with a sheet of wax paper. Draw a leaf pattern. Cut out four or five layers of one color of tissue. Place one leaf on the wax paper and cover the whole surface with the glue/water mixture. Place another tissue leaf on top of that and brush lightly with glue. Continue in the same manner until four or five layers have been built up. Allow plenty of time to dry (overnight or longer). Carefully peel the leaf away from the wax paper. With the pen or paint, lightly draw veins on the leaf. Make as many leaves as you would like, using the same method. Experiment by combining two different colors of art tissue. Use the leaves as a border around classroom windows, doors, or bulletin boards. Finished leaves can also be displayed altogether in a large basket.

Stalactites and Stalagmites (Chapter 20)

Kit described a beautiful cave with odd hanging shapes not unlike icicles. The correct term for these formations is "stalactites." A stalactite is formed from the build-up of mineral deposits from the limestone rock of the cave. Stalagmites are composed of the same minerals and look like upside-down icicles. Make stalactites and stalagmites with these easy directions.

Materials: 2 glass jars, Epsom salts (available at grocery stores and pharmacies), spoon, 2-foot (60 cm) long section of cotton string, scissors, water, 2 weights (washers, rocks, etc.), sheet of butcher paper

Directions: Spread the butcher paper on a flat surface. Fill both jars about half full with the Epsom salts. Add enough water to cover the salts and mix together. Place the jars on the paper and adjust as directed below.

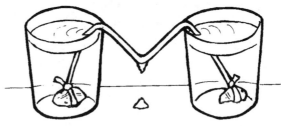

Tie a weight to each end of the string and place one washer in each jar. Move the jars so that the string hangs about 1 inch (2.54 cm) above the surface of the paper. Do not move the set up in any way. Crystals will start forming in about one week.

Learning Is Fun

When Kit tries to make learning fun for the children, her efforts are met with stern disapproval. About the only fun the children were allowed was chanting, usually about a Biblical saying. Later in the colonial era, other methods of learning were employed. Try out some of these methods with your class.

Spell It "Write"

Since communication was mostly written, much emphasis was placed on correct spelling. English is particularly tricky, however, because there is often more than one way to spell a particular sound. In the box below are some commonly misspelled words. This partial list was taken from *Stephen Caney's Kids' America* by Stephen Caney (Workman Publishing, 1978). Give the students a pretest to see how well they can spell these notorious trouble makers. Then assign the words for study in place of regular spelling words before giving a post test.

Commonly Misspelled Words

absence • accommodate • analyze • anonymous • business • conscience • conscious • definitely • disappoint • embarrass • fascinate • forty • grammar • height • hoarse • icicles • irresistible • jealousy • league • maneuver • misspelled • noticeable • occurrence • optimistic • parallel • phenomenon • principal • principle • privilege • receipt • seize • sergeant • sophomore • subtle

---

Spelling Bee

Everyone is familiar with the spelling bee, but it has lost favor because only good spellers participate. Here's an easy way to get everyone to join in. Divide the class into teams. The first person in the first team attempts to spell a given word. If the spelling is correct, that team earns a point and the first person goes to the end of the team's line. If the spelling is incorrect, the word passes on to the first person in the next group, and so on, until the word is spelled correctly. Keep playing until a team reaches 15 points.

A Twist of the Tongue

Colonial students were required to recite difficult, tongue-twisting sentences to improve diction. Have the students practice a tongue twister such as "Peter Piper" or one they have made. A great resource for tongue twisters is *The World's Toughest Tongue Twisters* by Joseph Rosenbloom (Sterling Publishing Company, 1986).

Rebus

Early American schools sometimes used the rebus as a teaching tool. A rebus is a word made up of pictures, symbols, letters, and numbers. Have the students make their own rebus words and sentences by cutting out and combining letters from newspapers and magazines. Write the following symbols on the board to help them get started.

---

a = a, hay, hey   B+4= before   B+Z = busy   C = see, sea

For more rebus ideas, see *Unriddling* by Alvin Schwartz (J.B. Lippincott, 1983).

A Colonial Ship

Directions: Pictured below is a cross-section of the *Susan Constant*, a typical sailing ship of the seventeenth century. Label the ship with the correct parts by unscrambling the letter groups below. Write the names on the corresponding lines below the ship. Here are some reference books to which you may refer: *Stephen Biesty's Incredible Cross-Sections* by Richard Platt, (Alfred A. Knopf, 1992), *Eyewitness Visual Dictionary: The Visual Dictionary of Ships and Sailing* (Dorling Kindersley, 1991), and *Inside Story: A 16th Century Galleon* by Richard Humble (Peter Bendrick Books, 1995).

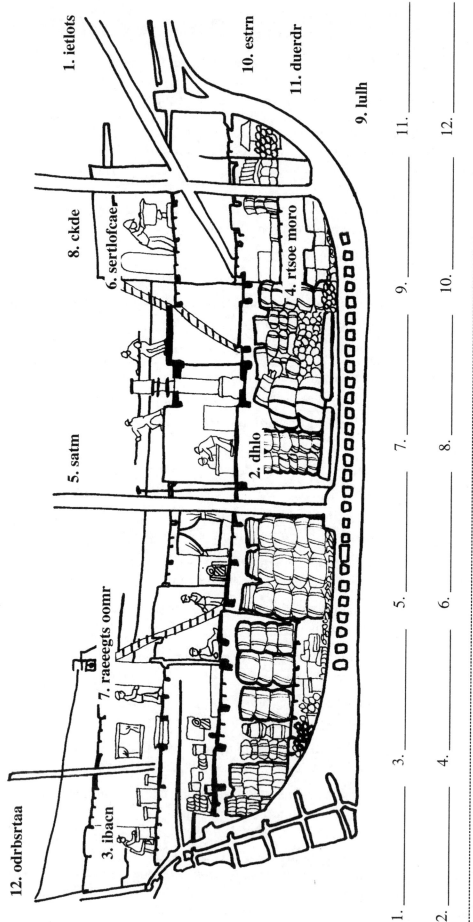

1. ietlots
2. dhlo
3. ibacn
4. odrbsrtaa
5. satm
6. sertlofcae
7. raeeegts oomr
8. ckde
9. lulh
10. estrn
11. duerdr
12. odrbsrtaa
14. rtsoe moro

1. _____
2. _____
3. _____
4. _____
5. _____
6. _____
7. _____
8. _____
9. _____
10. _____
11. _____
12. _____

Teacher: Fold under before copying

Answers: 1. toilets, 2. hold, 3. cabin, 4. store room, 5. mast, 6. forecastle, 7. steerage room, 8. deck, 9. hull, 10. stern, 11. rudder, 12. starboard

Character Quotes

Test students' knowledge of the characters with this quiz. Copy the characters from the box below onto the chalkboard. Read aloud a quote and allow groups of students to discuss and decide which character is being described—not who said the quote. Ask a group for their answer; discuss.

Governor Andros	Nat Eaton	Kit Judith	Matthew Wood	Mistress Eaton
William Ashby	Mercy	Goodwife Cruff	Adam Cruff	Reverend Bulkeley
Captain Talcott	Aunt Rachel	Prudence	Hannah Tupper	

1. "_____ eyed the girl before him. Quite plainly he had a distaste for the duty at hand, but his stern soldierly countenance did not soften."

2. "This _____ says right out that deeds signed by the Injuns are no better than scratches of a bear's paw! We are all to beg new grants for land we've bought and paid for."

3. "The child came slowly from behind the tree. She was thinner than ever, clad in a shapeless sacklike affair tied about her middle."_____

4. "What a child you are . . . Sometimes 'tis hard to believe you are sixteen." _____

5. "With dismay, Kit saw the captain's wife among the passengers preparing to disembark . . . They had shared the bond of being the only two women aboard the Dolphin." _____

6. "Then, as _____ stepped forward, one shoulder dipped and jerked back grotesquely, and Kit realized that she leaned on crutches."

7. "His wife had found her voice. 'Have ye lost your senses? The girl has bewitched you too!' " _____

8. "The clear white skin, the blue eyes under a dark fringe of lashes, the black hair that curled against her shoulders...this girl could have been the toast of a regiment!" _____

9. "For him it was enough simply to sit across the room and look at her . . . The most eligible bachelor in Wethersfield and handsome, actually, in his substantial way." _____

10. "She's not a witch, and you know it. She's a lonely old woman, and Judith, you couldn't help liking her if you knew her." _____

11. "Tonight she had understood for the first time what her aunt had seen in that fierce man to make her cross an ocean at his side. There was a sort of magnificence about him . . ." _____

12. "She has been insisting to my father that you are a witch. She says no respectable woman could keep afloat in the water like that." _____

13. "He is a hypocrite and a whited sepulcher!" Matthew's fist crashed down on the table. "And I'll have no more texts read at me in my own house!" _____

14. "What a touchy temper he had! She hadn't meant to insult his precious ship. Why did he deliberately turn everything to her disadvantage?"_____

Teacher: Fold under before copying
Answers: 1. Captain Talcott, 2. Governor Andros, 3. Prudence, 4. Kit, 5. Mistress Eaton, 6. Mercy, 7. Adam Cruff, 8. Judith, 9. William Ashby, 10. Hannah Tupper, 11. Matthew Wood, 12. Goodwife Cruff, 13. Reverend Bulkeley, 14. Nat Eaton

Barbados

Directions: With a partner, research and learn about Kit Tyler's native island of Barbados. Find and write the answers to the clues below. Then follow the instructions for labeling the map of Barbados. Use appropriate symbols to represent each answer on the map.

1. Large sugar cane farms are called _____. Draw four of these on the west side of the island.

2. A popular fish on the island is the _____ fish. Draw three of these fish in the waters off the southeast coast of Barbados.

3. Barbados lies NE of the country _____. Draw an arrow from Barbados to the direction of this country.

4. A major source of revenue of Barbados is _____. Draw an appropriate symbol for this industry on the southern edge of the island.

5. The highest mountain point of the island is _____. Draw and label the mountain in its correct location.

6. The national pastime on the island is _____. Draw an appropriate symbol for this game in the northwest corner of the island.

7. The capital of Barbados is _____. Write Barbados on the map and draw a star next to it.

8. An important crop and export of Barbados is _____. Draw three of these in the southwest section of the island.

9. _____ are a favorite root vegetable grown on the island. Draw six of these in the central part of the island.

10. Once used in the sugar cane industry, _____ still dot the island. Draw four of these on the island.

Atlantic Ocean

N
W ← → E
S

Caribbean Sea

Teacher: Fold under before copying.
Answers: 1. plantations, 2. flying, 3. Venezuela, 4. tourism, 5. Hillaby, 6. cricket, 7. Bridgetown, 8. sugar cane, 9. yams, 10. windmills.

The resource used for gathering the information on this page is *Barbados* by Merle Broberg (Chelsea House, 1989).

Meet Elizabeth George Speare

Born on November 21, 1908, in Melrose, Massachusetts, Elizabeth George Speare recalls her childhood as a happy time. Especially memorable were the large family reunions. At each one of these gatherings, Elizabeth and her favorite cousin would compare the latest stories they had written. They continued this tradition throughout their college years.

After graduating from Boston University with a Master of Arts degree, Elizabeth taught high school English from 1932 to 1936. Her first classroom assignment proved to be a challenging experience, teaching Shakespeare to a group of boys. Somehow she survived and learned two important things about herself. First, she found herself learning a lot from her students, and second, she discovered that she really enjoyed teaching.

When she married industrial engineer Alan Speare in 1936, she moved with him to Connecticut. The subsequent birth of her son and her daughter kept her busy with family activities such as scouting, PTA, and piano and dancing lessons for 15 years. Finally, the day came when Elizabeth decided it was time for her to write once again. Her first venture was a magazine article about family life. After all, it was what she knew best.

That changed, however, when she read a true story from New England history. Its heroine appealed to Elizabeth, and after a while she began creating and writing adventures about the girl. As chapters eventually evolved, Speare read them to her own daughter. That was the beginning of her book, *Calico Captive*.

Because she found researching and writing such an absorbing activity, Elizabeth continued to pursue her endeavor. Although she may not have written as many books as some authors, her work is highly regarded, and she has received prestigious honors; *The Witch of Blackbird Pond* and *The Bronze Bow* both received Newbery Medals.

Activities

- Writers are often advised to write about what they know best. Did Elizabeth follow this guideline? What do you know best? Write a story based on what you know best.

- Read *Calico Captive* or *The Bronze Bow*. Compare either novel to *The Witch of Blackbird Pond*.

- If Elizabeth George Speare was going to write a new novel, what suggestions would you give her? With the class brainstorm a list of colonial figures. Assign students to research one and list five interesting facts about that person. Include those facts in a letter suggesting an idea for a new novel.

The Thirteen Colonies

Virginia and Connecticut provided the settings for the two literature selections, *The Serpent Never Sleeps* and *The Witch of Blackbird Pond*, respectively. There were, of course, eleven more original settlements: Massachusetts, Maryland, New Hampshire, Rhode Island, New York, New Jersey, Pennsylvania, Delaware, Georgia, North Carolina, and South Carolina.

Have students investigate the founding of these colonies using the information on pages 53–57. Group the students, and then either have them read and discuss the paragraphs among themselves before entering into a whole class discussion, or assign each group a different colony and direct them to find additional facts. Compile their findings in a class "Colonial Facts Book."

Virginia

At age 27, Captain John Smith was chosen to head the London Company to settle America. Three ships with 144 men and boys aboard set out from London in December, 1606. Five months later, on May 14, 1607, they began the settlement which they called Jamestown.

It was an ill-fated attempt, however. Despite Smith's efforts to befriend the Indians, the settlers scoffed at his suggestions that they learn how to plant corn. Consequently, their food ran out and all but 38 people died. Four hundred new settlers arrived in 1609, but many were sick from eating spoiled food.

After suffering through the "starving time," the colonists wanted to leave. Soon after boarding a ship for England, 300 new colonists led by Lord De La Warr arrived. De La Warr instituted tough rules and punished anyone who would not work.

The situation finally took a turn for the better when colonist John Rolfe developed a tobacco that sold well in England. His subsequent marriage to Indian princess Pocahontas brought a peace to the settlement for many years.

Discussion

Over 5,000 people came to Virginia during an 18-year period; yet in 1624 only 1200 people were still there. What factors can be attributed to the loss of these colonists? What was the "starving time"?

Colonial Mini-Unit

Massachusetts

At one time, people in England were required to support the Church of England. One group, called Puritans, decided to simplify or "purify" the church. Some Puritans were jailed, and a few were even put to death for their beliefs.

Many left for Holland where they could practice their religion freely. But they worried that their children were learning Dutch ways, and so the group obtained a patent from the London Company to settle in Virginia. Instead, their ship landed somewhere off the coast of New England.

Miles Standish was chosen to lead this band of 50 men, 20 women, and 34 children. That winter, whole families died from the cold and illness, but in the spring the Indian named Squanto arrived and helped them. Not only could he speak English, but he showed the settlers how to trap, plant, and fish.

From 1621 to 1630, ships arrived with more settlers as well as the first cattle. By 1640, the New England population had swelled to 20,000.

Discussion
What factors contributed to the success of the Massachusetts colony? For what main reason was Massachusetts founded?

Maryland

George Calvert—Lord Baltimore—was the founder and owner of colonial Maryland. Unlike the mercenary London Company, his motives for establishing the colony were religious. Catholics in England could no longer openly attend mass and were fined for not belonging to the Church of England.

Fearing the power of the Puritans, Baltimore left England for the colonies. Although he died before reaching Maryland, his brother Cecil inherited the 10 million acres that encompassed Maryland, Delaware, Pennsylvania, West Virginia, and parts of Virginia. Two ships, the *Ark* and the *Dove*, carried 220 colonists, most of them servants who were Protestants.

An old Indian settlement was purchased by this group, and they set about building a fort, mill, and chapel. Although supplies were easily obtained from the Virginia settlements, new colonists already had been told what supplies they would need to bring with them. With the institution of the Toleration Act, Maryland became the first colony to grant religious freedom to its citizens.

Discussion
What was the Toleration Act? What prompted its passage?

The Thirteen Colonies *(cont.)*

Connecticut

Not everyone liked or agreed with the way Massachusetts Bay was being run, so they decided to found new settlements. One such dissenter was Reverend Thomas Hooker, a Puritan minister from Boston. Thirty-five families walked for two weeks before reaching the site that is now Hartford. Eventually, three towns joined together to form the colony of Connecticut in 1636.

Discussion
What were some Puritan rules that caused disagreement? What were some of Hooker's views?

New Hampshire

Two friends, Sir Fernando Gorges and John Mason, were granted the right to establish a colony in northern New England in 1622. This grant was called the "main" because it was on the main section of coastal land dotted by islands. The two men split up their holdings: Gorges took what would later become Maine (it was taken over by Massachusetts until 1820, when it became the 23rd state) while Mason kept what would become New Hampshire. In order to attract settlers, Gorges and Mason advertised in England.

Despite the response, the colony failed to survive as a separate entity; New Hampshire was taken back by the king for a number of years. In 1680, New Hampshire again became a separate colony.

Discussion
How do you think Maine got its name? (How did Gorges and Mason attract settlers? Was this a sensible idea?)

Rhode Island

Roger Williams was a likeable and brilliant Puritan minister, but he was not without his opponents. Williams preached against taking land from the Indians and thought that church and state should be separate. Both ideas were enough for the leaders of the Massachusetts Bay Colony to decide to banish him from the community.

Before Williams could be captured, though, he escaped. After purchasing land from the Indians, he founded Rhode Island. Soon, other rebels began to move there. Williams generously gave each settler five acres for gardening and six acres for cornfields. He also allowed everyone—not just Christians—to practice their own religions.

Discussion
The Puritans forced some Native Americans to become Christians. How do you think Williams felt about this? What is the most important idea professed by Williams?

The Thirteen Colonies *(cont.)*

New York

At one time in history, the Dutch had colonies all over the world. Their main goal was not to build settlements but to make money. What was then called New Amsterdam was no exception. In fact, they made what is probably the most famous land deal in history when Peter Minuit purchased Manhattan Island from the Indians for about $24 worth of trinkets. When the colony failed to attract Dutch settlers, they welcomed people from other countries and colonies. Peter Stuyvesant was named governor of the Dutch colony, but in 1664 the British took over and renamed it New York.

Discussion
Why didn't the Indians demand more for the property? Why didn't the colony attract many Dutch settlers?

New Jersey

Some of New York became New Jersey when the Duke of York (who later became James II, King of England) gave some of the land to two of his friends, George Carteret and John Berkeley in 1664. The settlement was named "New Jersey" after Carteret's home on the island of Jersey. A new charter was instituted which provided for freedom of religion, set up an assembly to represent the people, and gave the right to vote to every man. People flocked to the colony where Germans, Finns, Swedes, and English lived in harmony.

Discussion
Why do you think so many different people moved to New Jersey?

The Carolinas

Many problems faced the eight Lords Proprietor who were granted Carolina in 1663. The colony, which stretched from Virginia to Spanish Florida, was also claimed in part by Spain; new colonists might have to fight them for property. In addition, some of the land proved unhealthful for living, there were not enough supplies, and Indians forced some colonists off their claims. Then, in 1670, Charleston was established. From the start this settlement was a success, due in part to its busy port and wealthy, aristocratic leaders from Barbados. Black slaves were imported from the West Indies to work the rice plantations, and by the early 1700s slaves outnumbered whites in South Carolina.

North Carolina did not enjoy the early success of its southern neighbor. Colonists had to pay colony owners an annual fee, and there was no good seaport. Eventually, other colonies were created from the Carolina territory.

Discussion
What were some of the problems facing the new proprietors? Why was a good seaport so important?

Colonial Mini-Unit

The Thirteen Colonies *(cont.)*

Pennsylvania and Delaware

William Penn was born into an important and wealthy family, but he was not content to live that lifestyle. Instead, he became a champion of Quakers' rights. Beatings from his father, getting kicked out of college, and serving jail time did not deter his beliefs. Fortunately for William, his father had loaned a fortune to King Charles II. When the elder Penn died, William was owed the debt. But he didn't care for the money; he asked for a tract of land instead. What he received was a piece of land larger than all of England. The king named this property Pennsylvania ("Penn's woods").

Penn opened up the colony to people of all faiths, not just Quakers. He wanted the Quaker ideas of peace and goodness to prevail, as well as equal treatment for everyone and respect for all religions. It was in Pennsylvania that Indians were first treated as equals and objections were made to black slavery. In 1704, three counties in the southeastern part of Pennsylvania asked for and received a charter for a separate government. Seventy-two years later Delaware became an independent state.

Discussion: What is the difference between toleration and natural rights? What were some of the Quakers' beliefs?

Georgia

The state of Georgia was founded to help debtors get out of prison. At that time in England, anyone who could not pay his or her bills was thrown into a debtors' prison. With no way to earn money to repay the debts, many stayed in jail and died while imprisoned. After visiting a friend held in such a prison, James Oglethorpe, a member of Parliament, worked to change things.

Oglethorpe, along with some other lawmakers, asked the government to start a new colony for London's poor. The resulting colony, Georgia, was named in the king's honor and set up as a charity. In 1732, Oglethorpe and 35 families set sail from England for their new home. As soon as they landed, everyone set to work building houses. Heads of households were given free land and were not to lose their land because of debt. Oglethorpe quickly befriended the Indians, which saved the colony from future attacks. (The Native Americans there were still talking about the cruelties inflicted on their tribe by Hernando de Soto, who had marched his troops through the area in 1540.) In fact, the Indians even helped the colonists fight against later skirmishes with the Spaniards. Originally begun as a haven for London's poor, Georgia later welcomed people from many countries.

Discussion
What were conditions like in a debtors' prison? Why did Oglethorpe's ideals fail?

Colonial Mini-Unit

Colonial Life

Early settlers to America realized that they would have to make changes and adapt to new ways of living in their new habitat. Explore the following topics and learn about day-to-day life in early Colonial America.

✳ ✳ ✳ ✳ ✳ ✳ Housing ✳ ✳ ✳ ✳ ✳ ✳

At first, colonists had to make do with temporary shelters. English wigwams were dome-shaped structures patterned after the tents of the Algonquin Indians. These homes had one room with dirt floors and a very low doorway. Dutch settlers often built dugouts, which were pits dug into the side of a hill or into the ground. Southern colonists lived in lean-tos, which were sturdy planks positioned at an angle against a large tree or face of a cliff. Eventually, all of these primitive, temporary homes gave way to more permanent homes. A typical wooden house of the time consisted of a large room in which the floor was covered with wooden planks. A stone fireplace for heating and cooking took up one whole wall, and a loft provided a place for the children to sleep.

Research Ideas

- Draw the interior of a typical Dutch settlers' house; explain how it differed from the typical English house.
- Make a list of the different materials used in building these homes. Explain the advantages of each.

✳ ✳ ✳ ✳ ✳ ✳ Clothing ✳ ✳ ✳ ✳ ✳ ✳

Most people arriving in the early colonies came with only the clothes on their backs. For the most part, these clothes were ill-suited to the climate and the rugged life they faced. New clothes were made by hand at home by spinning and dyeing cloth. Natural dyes from tree bark, berries, and flowers provided color for the cloth. Leather was also used to make some articles of clothing such as hats and boots.

Research Ideas

- Compare the garments worn by the Native Americans with those worn by the early settlers. Tell what materials were used to construct the pieces of clothing.
- Explain how the clothing styles of the northern colonies differed from those in the southern colonies.

✳ ✳ ✳ ✳ ✳ ✳ Food ✳ ✳ ✳ ✳ ✳ ✳

Natural food resources were plentiful in Colonial America. Rivers and oceans yielded a variety of fish, while the woods were filled with deer, wild turkey, and game. Rich soil supported the growth of numerous fruits and vegetables. The first settlers, however, did not know how to farm the land. With the help of the Native Americans, the newcomers learned how to hunt, grow crops, and survive.

Colonial Life *(cont.)*

Research Ideas

- Make a list of the foods that the colonists brought with them.
- Corn was unknown to the colonists. Write a paragraph explaining the many uses the colonists found for corn in addition to being a food source.

✳ ✳ ✳ ✳ ✳ ✳ Work ✳ ✳ ✳ ✳ ✳ ✳

Daily life was a constant round of chores from cooking to building homes and furniture, growing food, tending the animals, weaving cloth, making soap and candles, and making utensils (buckets, brooms, spoons, etc.). No one was excluded from work.

Research Ideas

- Fold a sheet of paper in half. Label one side "men," the other "women." In each section, list the chores performed by each gender.
- Learn how the women made candles. Make a flow chart to show the process.

✳ ✳ ✳ ✳ ✳ ✳ Schooling ✳ ✳ ✳ ✳ ✳ ✳

Ordinarily, the only formal schooling most Puritan children received was that of a two-year dame school. Some northern colonies offered another level of schooling beyond the dame school called "common schools." Common schools were nothing more than dark, one-room buildings. There were no chalkboards, maps, or textbooks. Written lessons had to be written on tree bark, using a lump of lead or a goose quill pen.

Research Ideas

- Discipline included these harsh methods: whipping with a birch rod, being placed in stocks for hours, wearing a dunce cap. Conduct a class debate on whether these disciplines are effective or not.
- Make a chart to compare the one-room school of yesterday with the schools of today. Include topics such as teaching aids, rules and discipline, and teachers.

✳ ✳ ✳ ✳ ✳ ✳ Pastimes ✳ ✳ ✳ ✳ ✳ ✳

Life was harsh, and people needed some time to have fun. Even the fiercely religious Puritans allowed their members to seek some amusements. Children typically played games such as tag, hide and seek, and blindman's buff. In addition, boys played with tops and marbles while girls embroidered samplers and played with dolls.

Research Ideas

- Adult men enjoyed amusements such as bowling, nine pins, and quoits. Except for ice skating, women did not participate in such events. Learn what amusements they did enjoy.
- Black slaves and Native Americans had their own pastimes. Write a report explaining what these two groups did for relaxation and amusement.

Colonial Mini-Unit

Colonial Quiz

How well do you know your colonies? Find out by taking the quiz below. Refer to the map on page 61 and match the names and phrases to the correct colony. Write the name of the colony on the lines provided.

1. _____ named after Lord De La Warr

2. _____ James Oglethorpe and debtor's prison

3. _____ the Mayflower Compact

4. _____ Roger Williams and other rebels

5. _____ colony run by Catholics

6. _____ pirate Anne Bonney

7. _____ John Rolfe and Pocahontas

8. _____ Penn's Woods

9. _____ the patron system

10. _____ Charleston, the busiest port in the South

11. _____ Reverend Thomas Hooker

12. _____ Samoset helped the Pilgrims

13. _____ originally part of Pennsylvania

14. _____ the Toleration Act

15. _____ many of its leaders were from Barbados

16. _____ Quakers and brotherly love

17. _____ named after King George II

18. _____ Salem witch trials

19. _____ Peter Minuit's land deal

20. _____ named after a county in England

- -

Teacher: Fold under before copying this page.
Answers: 1. Delaware, 2. Georgia, 3. Massachusetts, 4. Rhode Island, 5. Maryland, 6. North Carolina, 7. Virginia, 8. Pennsylvania, 9. New York, 10. South Carolina,
11. Connecticut, 12. Massachusetts, 13. Delaware, 14. Maryland, 15. South Carolina,
16. Pennsylvania, 17. Georgia, 18. Massachusetts, 19. New York, 20. New Hampshire

Colonial Mini-Unit

Colonial Quiz *(cont.)*

Directions: Use the map below to complete the quiz on page 60.

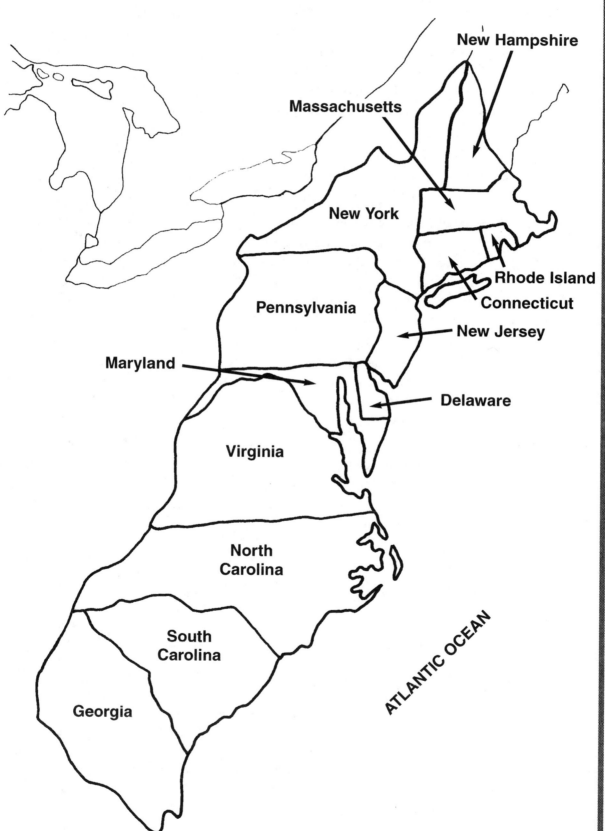

New Hampshire

Massachusetts

New York

Rhode Island

Connecticut

Pennsylvania

New Jersey

Maryland

Delaware

Virginia

North Carolina

South Carolina

Georgia

ATLANTIC OCEAN

Colonial Mini-Unit

Culminating Activities

Wrap up the thematic unit on Colonial America with any of the projects on this page. Divide the students into five groups and assign a project to each.

> You are the leader of a group that is dissatisfied with recently enacted government policies. You find these rules both intolerable and against your beliefs. All offenders will be banished from the community. Your group decides to relocate to a place where you can be free from these rules.

- Determine where your group will move (any place in the world) and explain why you chose that particular destination.

- Make a list of the government policies with which you are dissatisfied.

- What rules will you initiate in your new community? Write a charter for your colony.

- Draw and label a map of the 13 colonies. (A blank United States map is provided on page 79.) Outline the Middle colonies with brown crayon or colored pencil, the New England colonies with orange, and the Southern colonies with green. Label each with its founding leader(s), religious affiliation(s), and name of the country origins of its settlers. Choose one of the three areas (Middle, New England, Southern) and explain why you would prefer to live there rather than either of the other two.

- Compare life among the Middle, New England, and Southern colonies with a three-way Venn diagram or chart. Some topics to include are slavery, religion, living conditions, crops grown, soil conditions, dress and fashions, religious toleration, voting rights, witchcraft, entertainments, farms and plantations, leaders, and significant contributions to society.

- Some colorful characters are associated with the early days of the 13 original colonies. Choose one of the following and write a news story for your local paper. Be sure to include information from each of the "5 Ws" (who, what, where, when, why) plus how.

Peter Stuveysant	Cotton Mather
Samoset	Benjamin Franklin
Tituba	Olaudah Equiano
Sir Edmund Andros	Mary Read
Anne Hutchinson	Anne Bonney
Opechancanough	

- Southern plantations were self-sufficient. Each one had its own gardens to grow fruits and vegetables, acreage for livestock, and fields where crops were grown. In addition, there were numerous buildings on the premises to house all of the supporting services. These included servants' quarters, a school house, blacksmith's shed, stable, and the main living quarters. Draw a map of a typical plantation. Label each building and tell what work went on there. Describe life there for a colonial child.

Colonial Mini-Unit

Annotated Bibliography

Students will find the following books useful for researching material and locating information for the various projects and activities in this Colonial America mini-unit. Look for them in your school or local library and in the children's section of bookstores.

Colonial American Home Life by John F. Warner (Franklin Watts, 1993)

What was it like to be a child in Colonial America? How did people eat and dress? How long did they attend school? What chores did they have? What foods did they eat and how were meals cooked? These and many other questions are answered in this thorough, unique picture of the way people lived in Colonial America.

Eating the Plates: A Pilgrim Book of Food and Manners by Lucille Recht Penner (Macmillan Publishing Company, 1991)

This book contains a wealth of surprising information. Did you know that the English did not like fruits or vegetables? Or that no one had his or her own plate? Or that almost no one used a fork? Children and adults alike will delight in the amazing facts presented throughout this most fascinating book.

The Explorers and Settlers, edited by Carter Smith (The Millbrook Press, 1991)

This book presents an historical perspective through the lives of the explorers. Maps, pictures, and numerous time lines of major events provide a clear picture of the beginnings of America.

The First Passage: Blacks in the Americas by Colin A. Palmer (Oxford University Press, 1995)

In this authoritative text, the roots of the African American are traced from Africa to the American colonies. Their tragic capture and enslavement, the ordeal of the Atlantic Ocean crossing, and the subsequent loss of family and friends are all thoroughly explored. Pictures and diagrams further help humanize a most dehumanizing situation.

Founding the American Colonies by Diana Reische (Franklin Watts, 1989)

Opening with the story of the Virginia colony, this book then progresses in chronological order to the founding of the remaining colonies. This is a concise text with some beautiful pictures interspersed throughout the pages.

If You Lived in Colonial Times by Ann McGovern (Scholastic, 1964)

The question-and-answer format is a sure winner. Everything you want to know about colonial times is asked and answered here.

Making Thirteen Colonies by Joy Hakim (Oxford University Press, 1993)

Altogether there are ten books in this series, "A History of Us." This is Book Two in which the story of the first settlers to America is told. Pictures, diagrams, and sidebars of information complement the engrossing text.

A Colonial Word Search

Test your knowledge of daily life in the thirteen colonies. Use these clues to find the twenty words in the word search.

1. the only sport in which women could participate
2. metal from which some plates and cups were made
3. the only utensil used for eating
4. common method of punishment for criminals
5. type of home built by early Dutch settlers
6. plant used in making candles
7. girls embroidered these
8. they sold wares and spread news
9. cloth spun from the flax plant
10. dish made from wood or stale bread

11. children ages six to eight attended these
12. plant grown for its blue dye
13. windows were made by soaking cloth in this oil
14. a basic ingredient of soap
15. game in which metal rings were tossed at an iron stake
16. one page of letters fastened to a wooden frame
17. waist-length jacket worn by men
18. fried cornmeal bread
19. type of house with sloping roof
20. day of worship

o	a	l	p	p	l	i	n	s	e	e	d	m	n	i
s	t	o	s	e	y	c	u	t	a	p	i	h	d	n
f	x	h	r	w	e	e	s	i	m	p	e	u	u	d
o	o	t	e	t	v	s	t	o	c	k	s	o	g	i
e	m	a	l	e	a	k	e	u	b	o	c	f	o	g
y	a	b	d	r	e	a	d	q	h	o	g	e	u	o
r	t	b	d	b	a	t	d	o	u	b	l	e	t	w
r	r	a	e	x	u	i	h	e	u	n	e	n	i	l
e	e	s	p	o	o	n	v	l	c	r	b	b	n	j
b	n	d	e	b	e	g	d	c	m	o	o	d	a	a
y	c	z	r	t	p	f	m	y	j	h	q	z	x	o
a	h	e	f	l	j	o	h	n	n	y	c	a	k	e
b	e	g	d	a	m	e	s	c	h	o	o	l	u	k
r	r	h	t	s	a	m	p	l	e	r	s	n	r	l

- -

Teacher: Fold under before copying this page.
Answers: 1. ice skating, 2. pewter, 3. spoon, 4. stocks, 5. dugout, 6. bayberry, 7. samplers, 8. peddlers, 9. linen, 10. trencher, 11. dame school, 12. indigo, 13. linseed, 14. lye, 15. quoits, 16. hornbook, 17. doublet, 18. johnnycake, 19. saltbox, 20. Sabbath

Time Traveling

Pretend you were on the scene as these historical events were unfolding. Try to imagine being inside the mind of a Colonial American as you write about the following situations.

- A neighbor has been accused of practicing witchcraft, and now authorities are searching for him or her. Make a "Wanted" poster that includes the following information: a mug drawing of the neighbor, physical description, list of crimes, reward offered.

- Squanto has befriended your colony and taught members how to hunt, fish, and plant. Write Squanto a thank-you note for all of his help.

- You have just been captured from your native Africa by people who speak a strange language. Write a diary entry about that fateful day.

- Fall is a colorful and beautiful season in New England. Describe the sights and smells that greet you during your first autumn in these colonies.

- Corn is a dietary staple in the colonies, and your mother knows fourteen different ways to prepare it. Write a recipe for a new corn dish you would like her to cook.

- Pocahontas does not enjoy wearing strange clothing and being forced to practice a new religion. Write a poem to describe how she feels in captivity.

- Peter Minuit has just offered your people some trinkets for Manhattan Island. Your tribe agrees to the deal. Explain why you think your tribe got the better of the bargain.

- Life in the southern colonies is far more genteel than that of the northern colonies. Write a letter to your northern cousin telling him or her about life in the South.

- As the new schoolmistress, you want to make learning fun for the children. Make up three different chants to help the children learn their lessons.

- A time machine has enabled you to go back in time to Colonial America. You can only take three modern items with you to leave with the colonists. Write a story about your visit and explain what items you chose to give the colonists. Be sure to explain your reasons for your choices.

- Everyone is required to attend Sunday services for two hours on Sunday morning and two hours that same afternoon. Make a list of all the things you do to keep from falling asleep during the long sermons.

- During mealtimes you have to keep quiet, and as a child you must stand throughout a meal. Write a book of manners you must obey.

Information Math

All of the math problems on this page are composed of tidbits of information about the early history of the American colonies. Make a transparency of this page for the overhead projector and conduct a whole group oral lesson. Ask students to identify the following information in each problem before they perform any work: what the problem is asking; what information, if any, is irrelevant; what operation(s) is needed to solve the problem; how to solve the problem. For your reference, answers are included at the bottom of this page.

1. The colonial period extends from the beginning of Jamestown in 1607 until the Declaration of Independence was signed in 1776. How long was the colonial period?

2. On March 22, 1622, Chief Opechancanough and his warriors attacked Jamestown, killing a third of the 1,200 inhabitants. How many Jamestown settlers were killed? How many settlers remained?

3. The first few years in the new colonies were extremely difficult. Four out of five of the first 10,000 settlers died soon after arrival in Virginia. How many of those first settlers died? What percentage is that?

4. The winter of 1609-1610 is known as the Starving Time. By the spring of 1610, of 500 original people only 60 were still alive. How many people had died? What percentage of people were still alive?

5. By the year 1725, about 75,000 blacks were living in the American colonies. Sixty-five years later there were more than 10 times that number.

   What year was it 65 years later? How many more blacks were there then than in 1725?

6. Virginia's capital city of Williamsburg was a small town of 2,000 people, half of them African Americans. When the House of Burgesses was in session, though, the population doubled. How many of the town's inhabitants were not African American? What was the population during the House sessions?

7. Between 1630 and 1640, about 20,000 Puritans set sail for New England. On average, how many Puritans set sail each year from 1630 to 1640?

Teacher: Fold under before making transparency.

Answers
1. 1776 - 1607 = 169
2. $\frac{1}{3}$ x 1,200 = 400 or 1,200 divided by 3 = 400
   1,200 - 400 = 800
3. $\frac{4}{5}$ x 10,000 = 8,000; $\frac{4}{5}$ = 80%

4. 500 - 60 = 440; $\frac{60}{500}$ = .12 = 12%
5. 1725 + 65 = 1790 10 x 75,000 = 675,000
6. $\frac{1}{2}$ x 2,000 = 1,000 or 2,000 divided by 2 = 1,000; 2 x 2,000 = 4,000
7. 1640 - 1630 = 10; 20,000 divided by 10 = 2,000

Charting the Slave Trade

During the period from 1526 to 1870, millions of slaves were shipped from Africa to various North and South American countries. Study the graph below, and then answer the questions that follow on the lines provided.

Europe	← 200,000
Spanish America	1,552,000
Brazil	3,642,000
British Caribbean	1,665,000
Br. N. Am. & United States	399,000
French America	1,600,000
Dutch America	500,000
Danish West Indies	← 20,000

1. Which country received the most slaves? The least? _____

_____

2. How many more slaves were sent to French America than to Europe? _____

3. Which two countries have the most slaves? What is the difference between these numbers? _____

_____

4. What two countries have an almost equal number of slaves? _____

_____

5. How many slaves were exported altogether? Round your answer to the nearest million. _____

_____

Teacher: Fold under before copying this page.

Figures for this graph were taken from the text of *Making Thirteen Colonies* by Joy Hakim (Oxford University Press, 1993).

Answers: 1. Brazil and Danish West Indies, 2. 1,400,000, 3. Brazil and British Caribbean—1,977,000, 4. French America and Spanish America, 5. 10,000,000

Science and the Colonies

During the Colonial period, scientists were observing, calculating, and theorizing about a number of subjects. Read about three of the most famous scientists of the era. All of them changed the scientific laws of their day and influenced even more exciting advances in the current century. Learn something about them and their work with the biographical sketches and follow-up activities on pages 68–70.

Galileo Galilei

Known simply as Galileo, this Italian revolutionized the world of science with his studies which showed that the earth and other planets orbit about the sun. At that time, it was a widely held belief that the earth was stationary and the planets orbited the sun. In addition, Galileo discovered the laws of falling bodies and the law governing how a pendulum works.

Activities

- Galileo used square and triangular numbers to explain the theory of falling bodies. Find out the difference between square and triangular numbers. Write the first ten square numbers and the first ten triangular numbers; make models of each number.

- Galileo was the first to use the telescope to study the planets. He discovered sunspots and found that Venus has phases just like our moon. Write a description of a sunspot. Draw and label the phases of the moon.

- Observations made of the back-and-forth swinging of a lamp led Galileo to the discovery of how pendulums work. Observe the pendulum action of a swing in the playground or construct a pendulum.

Resources on Galileo

Galileo and the Magic Numbers by Sidney Rosen (Little, 1958)

Great Lives: Invention and Technology by Milton Lomask (Charles Scribner's Sons, 1991)

Focus on Inventors by Mary Ellen Sterling (Teacher Created Resources #496) This book gives directions for a classrooom pendulum and other Galileo-related projects.

Science and the Colonies *(cont.)*

Isaac Newton

Interestingly enough, Isaac Newton was born the same year that Galileo died—1642. Newton's prism experiments were what brought him early fame, but what he is most remembered for these days is his book *Principia Mathematica (Mathematics Principles)*. In it, he formulated the laws of gravity and planetary motion. Newton also created the reflecting telescope and developed calculus.

Activities

Gravity is a force created by the earth's pull on all bodies. This force is concentrated in each body at its center of gravity. Have students find their own center of gravity as they walk on a balance beam or try to stand still on one foot.

There are three laws of motion. The first law states that if something is not moving, it will not start until something causes it to begin moving. Demonstrate this with a skateboard. Place it on the ground and have students make observations about its movement. Now, push the skateboard towards a wall to demonstrate the second law of motion—once something is moving it will not stop until something causes it to stop. When the skateboard hits the wall and bounces back, students will observe the third law of motion: For every action there is an equal and opposite reaction.

> If something is not moving, it will not start moving unless something causes it to begin moving.

> Once something is moving, it will not stop until something causes it to stop.

> For every action there is an equal and opposite reaction.

Resources on Isaac Newton

Isaac Newton, Reluctant Genius by D. C. Ipsen (Enslow, 1985)

Janice Van Cleave's Gravity by Janice Van Cleave (John Wiley & Sons, Inc., 1993) This book is full of interesting facts and experiments.

Janice Van Cleave's Physics for Every Kid by Janice Van Cleave (John Wiley & Sons, Inc., 1991) Experiments with a pendulum and gravity are included.

Science and the Colonies *(cont.)*

—— Benjamin Franklin ——

Among other things, Benjamin Franklin was a statesman, writer, scientist, and inventor. Some of his inventions include the lightning rod, Franklin stove, and bifocals, but there was even more to the American Benjamin Franklin. His kite flying experiment was legendary. Through it, he showed a very important concept—that lightning and electricity are the same thing.

Activities

Static electricity is electricity at rest. Charges stay still and do not move along wires. Demonstrate the effects of static electricity with either of these two experiments.

1. Rub a balloon against your clothing. Stick the balloon on a wall. Why does it stay there? First, you need to know three facts:

- Electrons have a negative charge.
- A negative and a positive charge attract one another.
- Like charges (two negatives or two positives) repel or push away from one another.

Now, electrons have rubbed off from your clothing onto the balloon, giving the balloon a negative charge. As these negative charges from the balloon approach the wall, negative charges in the wall are repelled. This leaves a positive charge where the balloon touches the wall. Since a positive and a negative attract, the balloon sticks to the wall.

2. Cut up some tiny pieces of aluminum foil or tissue and place the pieces on a table or flat surface. Run a comb through your hair. Hold the comb above the paper pieces. Watch as the paper moves up toward the comb.

Resources on Benjamin Franklin

Ben and Me by Robert Lawson (Little, Brown and Company, 1951)

Electricity. A Creative Hands-On Approach to Science by Wendy Baker and Andrew Haslan (Macmillan Publishing Company, 1993)

General Resources for pages 68-70

Beakman's Book of Dead Guys and Gals of Science by Luann Colombo (Andrews and McMeel, 1994). A hilarious yet informative look at the lives of some important scientists.

Focus on Inventors by Mary Ellen Sterling (Teacher Created Resources #496)

Hands-On Projects

For a change of pace, give students a choice of any of the following hands-on projects. While research is required for most, the typical report or research paper has been replaced here with a livelier activity.

- Iroquois Indians lived in large community houses called "longhouses." Find out the typical dimensions of a longhouse and learn how one was constructed. Make a scale model of a longhouse.

- Compare the adult amusements of the Europeans (such as bowling, quoits, dances) with those of the Native Americans (such as canoe races, hoops, lacrosse). Invent a new game for children, using materials available in Colonial America.

- With a partner, write an agreement between a master and his indentured servant. Sign and tear the paper in half so that each of you has an indentation that can fit into the other piece.

- Algonquins lived in dome-shaped wigwams covered with tree bark or animal skins. Compare these wigwams with the wigwams built by the early English settlers. Draw a picture or make a model of a wigwam.

- Research the slave trade and learn how natives were brought from the islands to the colonies to help on large plantations. Explain what fears the slaves might have had. Describe their ocean journey in a cinquain. (See page 40 to find out one way to write a cinquain.)

- Study the process of colonial tobacco farming; make a flow chart to show how it is grown and harvested.

- The Native Americans' greatest gift to the settlers was corn. Draw, color, and label an ear of corn.

- Study the bayberry plant and research how it was first used in candlemaking. Draw and color a picture of a bayberry plant. Write its scientific name. List some other uses for the plant.

- Compare life in Colonial America with life among pioneers in the early 1800s. List those things which were the same and those that were different. Determine how much life had changed and improved between those two eras. Further compare life in Colonial America to life now. List the improvements that we now enjoy in our daily lives.

- Examine an actual supply list of items that men were required to bring with them to Virginia. Choose the top ten items you would bring. Explain your choices. If you could bring only one thing, what would it be and why?

- Construct a time line to show historical events as they occurred during the Colonial period.

Triangular Trade

Look carefully at the map. Notice the three-sided figures made by the lines between the colonies, Europe, and Africa. The resulting triangles made up what is known as "triangular trade." All of the countries were interconnected by slave trade. In addition, goods from the colonies were traded in England. From there, ships traveled to Africa to trade goods for slaves. Then ships went back to the West Indies and the home port. To help you learn more about this triangular trade, follow the directions below.

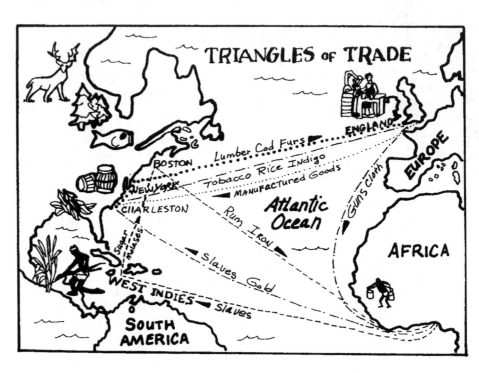

Then use the map to help you determine which goods were imported and exported among countries. Read each clue and write *imported* or *exported* on the lines provided.

1. Rum and iron were _____ to Africa.

2. Slaves were _____ to the West Indies.

3. Lumber, cod, and furs were _____ by England.

4. Sugar and molasses were _____ to Boston from the West Indies.

5. Manufactured goods were _____ by the colonies from England.

6. Gold and slaves were _____ from Africa to the colonies.

7. Tobacco, rice, and indigo were _____ from Charleston to England.

8. Guns and cloth were _____ by England.

- -

Teacher: Fold over before copying this page.

Answers: 1) exported, 2) exported, 3) imported, 4) exported, 5) imported, 6) exported, 7) exported, 8) exported

In the Meantime

The colonial period lasted from 1607 to 1776. It was a time of rapid growth and monumental changes. During this time frame, other equally important events were transpiring in other countries worldwide. Read the description of the events below. Fill in the blanks with the following terms.

> steam engine • artist • clock • Catholics • Spain • pendulum • playwright • Australia
> composer • Dutch • comet • Bible • blood • Thirty Years' War • telescope

1. **1628:** Circulation of the _____ is discovered by William Harvey of England.

2. **1611:** A new English translation of the _____, authorized by King James, is published.

3. **1642:** Italian mathematician and physicist Galileo discovers how the _____ works.

4. **1609:** Henry Hudson, sailing for the _____ , first sails up the Hudson River which is named in his honor.

5. **1682:** English astronomer Edmund Halley first observes the _____ now named after him.

6. **1641:** _____ revolt in Ireland; 30,000 Protestants are massacred.

7. **1616:** Poet and _____ William Shakespeare, the greatest writer in Elizabethan times, dies.

8. **1633:** France declares war on _____.

9. **1656:** Dutchman Christian Huygens invents the first pendulum _____.

10. **1764:** Austrian _____ Wolfgang Mozart writes his first symphony at age eight.

11. **1648:** The Peace of Westphalia ends the _____.

12. **1768:** British Captain James Cook explores the coast of _____ and New Zealand.

13. **1660:** Diego Velazquez, an outstanding Spanish _____, dies.

14. **1775:** Scottish inventor Isaac Watt develops an improved _____.

15. **1668:** Sir Isaac Newton invents the reflecting _____ .

Teacher: Fold under before copying this page.

Answers: 1. blood 2. Bible 3. pendulum 4. Dutch 5. comet 6. Catholics 7. playwright 8. Spain 9. clock 10. composer 11. Thirty Years' War 12. Australia 13. artist 14. steam engine 15. telescope

Bulletin Board Ideas

To help set the stage for the study of Colonial America, you may want to prepare a Colonial-themed bulletin board. Enlist students to help you with the enlargement and assembly. Use pages 75-77 as needed. Labels for the colonies are provided on page 78. You may wish to use them with these activities.

Set the Stage. Cover the background of the bulletin board with a dark material made from butcher paper, gift wrapping paper, or burlap. Enlarge the patterns of the thirteen colonies on pages 75-77 using an overhead or an opaque projector (or have it done at a copy shop).

Assemble and staple the colonies to the bulletin board background. Label the colonies. Write pertinent information on index cards and connect them to the corresponding colony with a length of yarn.

Reusable Bulletin Board. Assemble all bulletin board pieces on a large sheet of poster board and laminate. Write on the laminated surface with water-based wipe-off pens. Students can practice identifying and labeling the colonies and writing pertinent information on each colony.

Separate Display. Assign a different colony to each pair or small group. Have them enlarge their colony's outline with the use of an overhead or opaque projector. Cut out the shape and outline with black marking pen. Use the center section for writing a report or recording information about the colony. Attach the completed colonies to a classroom wall.

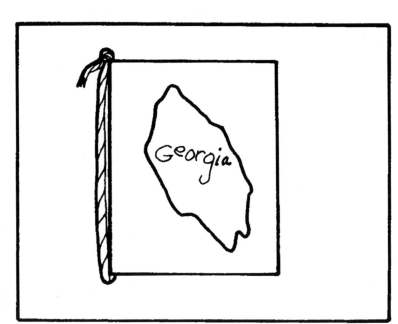

Colonial File Folders. Enlarge each colony enough to almost fill the front of a file folder. Cut out around the outline. Place the colony pattern on the folder and glue it in place. Students can use their folders for writing biographical sketches of important people in that colony, creative writing assignments, or labeling a topographical map of the colony.

Boxes of Colonies. Create a colonial box. Tape a small packing box. Paint the whole surface with a dark color (blue works well) or cover with butcher paper, newspaper, or wrapping paper. Assign each group a different colony and have them use the appropriate pattern to make an outline of their colony. Attach the outline to one of the faces of the box. Information to include on the other faces include a time line of events in the founding of the colony, biographical sketches of important people, a map of the colony, lists of its imports and exports, and prominent political and religious beliefs.

Colony Patterns

See page 74 for suggested uses.

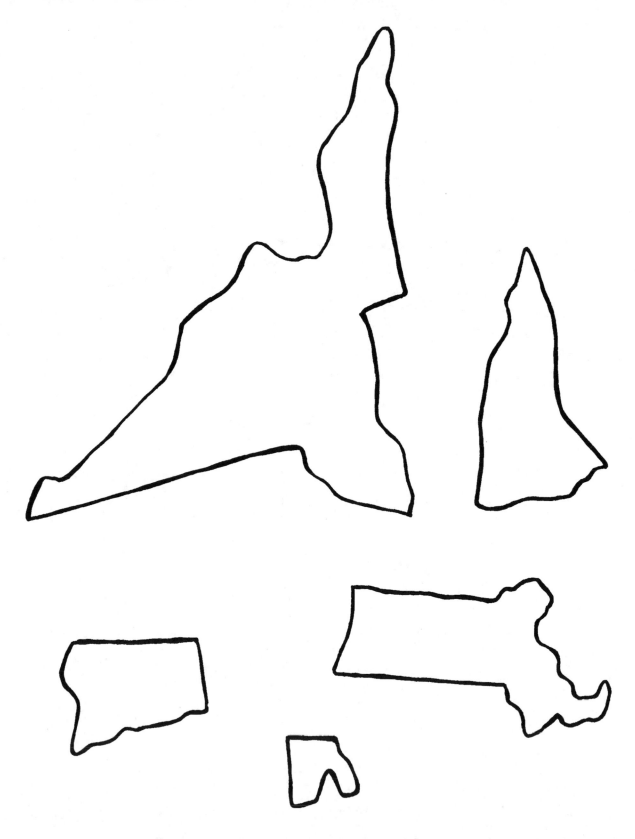

Colony Patterns *(cont.)*

See page 74 for suggested uses.

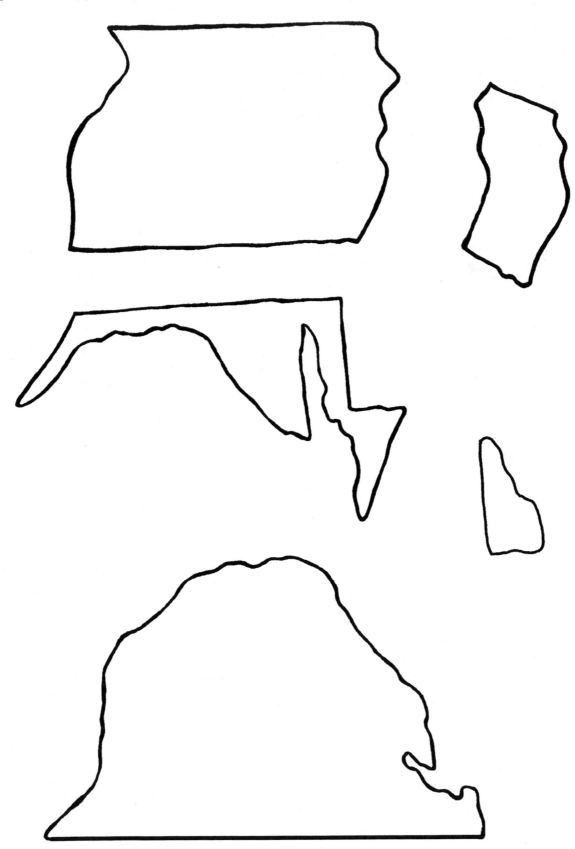

Colony Patterns *(cont.)*

See page 74 for suggested uses.

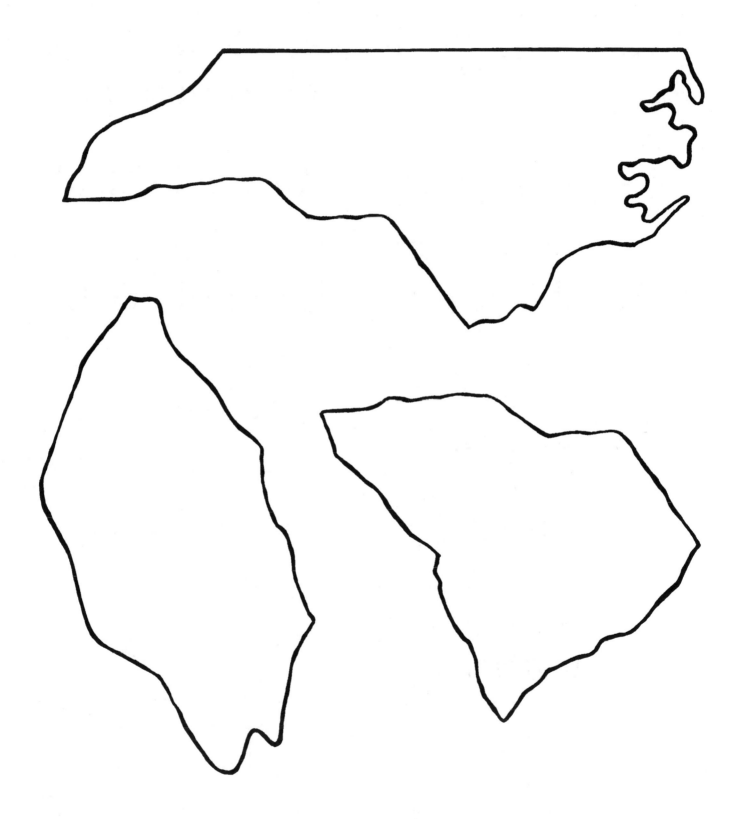

Colony Labels *(cont.)*

See page 74 for suggested uses.

New York	New Hampshire
Connecticut	Rhode Island
New Jersey	Pennsylvania
North Carolina	Delaware
Virginia	Maryland
South Carolina	Georgia

Massachusetts

Blank United States Map

Teacher Note: This map can be used for a variety of activities throughout the unit.

Bibliography

Historical Literature

Bradford, William. *Homes in the Wilderness*: *A Pilgrim's Journal of Plymouth Plantation in 1620*. Linnet, 1988.

Caney, Stephen. *Stephen Caney's Kids' America*. Workman Publishing, 1978.

Clapp, Patricia. *Constance: A Story of Early Plymouth*. Penguin Press, 1987.

_____*Witches' Children: A Story of Salem*. Penguin Press, 1987.

Daugherty, James. *Landing of the Pilgrims*. Random House, 1987.

Fleischman, Paul. *Saturnalia*. Harper, 1990.

Fritz, Jean. *The Double Life of Pocahontas*. Putnam, 1983.

Gilgen, Elizabeth. *Anne Hutchinson*. Chelsea House, 1991.

Gleiter, Jan and Kathleen Thompson. *Pocahontas*. Raintree Childrens' Books, 1985.

Kay, Alan N. *Jamestown Journey*. Thomas Publications, 1992.

Knight, James E. *Adventures in Colonial America: Jamestown, New World Adventure*. Troll Associates, 1982.

Lobel, Arnold. *On the Day Peter Stuyvesant Sailed into Town*. Harper, 1971.

Madison, Arnold. *How the Colonists Lived*. McKay, 1981.

McGovern, Ann. *If You Sailed on the Mayflower in 1620*. Scholastic, 1991.

Smith, Carter. *The Jamestown Colony*. Silver Burdett Press, 1991.

Speare, Elizabeth George. *Calico Captive*. Houghton Mifflin, 1957.

Warner, John F. *Colonial American Home Life*. Franklin Watts, 1993.

Waters, Kate. *Sarah Morton's Day, A Day in the Life of a Pilgrim Girl*. Scholastic, Inc., 1989.

Wisler, G. Clifton. *This New Land*. Walker, 1987.

Multimedia

CD-Source Book of American History. Macintosh/Windows. Candlelight Publishing, 800-677-3045 This handy reference helps link historical events and figures.

Cobblestone CD/ROM Library. An American history reference based on the pages of *Cobblestone*. Call 1-800-821-0115.

Where in America's Past Is Carmen San Diego? Broderbund. Call 1-800-521-6263 for more information and system requirements.

The Colonial Way of Life, 25 minutes. McGraw Hill Films, 1970

Colonial America, 20 minutes. ABC Films, 1975.

Colonial America, The Beginnings, 25 minutes. McGraw Hill Films, 1970.

The Witches of Salem, 34 minutes. Learning Corporation of America, 1972.

Cobblestone Magazine, 7 School Street, Peterborough, NH 03458-1454.

"The Witches of Connecticut" by Lawrence Cortesi, Oct., 1986, pp.22-24.

Jamestown, April, 1994. Also, *Colonial Craftsmen* (June, 1990), *Old Sturbridge Village: A Living History* (February, 1982), *Witchcraft* (October, 1986).

Teacher Created Resources

#364 Literature and Critical Thinking (contains unit on *The Witch of Blackbird Pond*)

#402 The Sign of the Beaver (Literature Unit)

#404 The Witch of Blackbird Pond (Literature Unit)

#472 Learning Through Literature: U. S. History

#582 Thematic Unit —U.S. Constitution